8 KEYS
TO
EXCEPTIONAL SELLING

Mike Rodriguez

8 KEYS TO EXCEPTIONAL SELLING

Become the Salesperson You Were Meant to Be

By Mike Rodriguez

Tribute Publishing

2014

Copyright © 2014
Mike Rodriguez
Frisco, Texas

Tribute Publishing

8 KEYS to Exceptional Selling
First Edition September 2014

All Worldwide Rights Reserved
ISBN: 978-0-9906001-0-7
ISBN: 978-0-9906001-1-4

All Rights Reserved. No part of this book may be reproduced, stored in a retrieval system, or transmitted, in any form, or by any means, electronic, mechanical, recorded, photocopied, or otherwise, without the prior written permission of the copyright owner, except by a reviewer who may quote brief passages in a review.

Printed in the United States of America.

TO BONNIE
The love of my life.
Thank you for believing in me
and never giving up on me.
I will love you always and forever.

To My Beautiful, Kind and Smart Daughters
Lauren
Lexi
Linsey
Leia
London
God has amazing opportunities awaiting each of you.
I'm so proud of you and I love you so much.

CONTENTS

Dedication xiii
Foreword xvii

KEY 1 – Everything Starts with YOU 1
   You MUST have a Positive Attitude to Succeed 4
   The Positive Factor 7
   The Pain of Change 8
   You Must Know Your WHY 13
   Your CORE 4 – Who is Influencing Your Life? 14
   Be Genuine and Sincere 18
   Be Accountable 19
   Know what you are Selling 21
   Dress for Success 22
   Have Integrity 24

KEY 2 – EMBRACE the Art & Science of Sales 27
   The Art of Sales 28
   The Science of Sales 30

KEY 3 – THINK About Your Prospects 35
   Never Negotiate with Fear or Mediocrity 38
   Knowledge and Strategies Must be Internalized 40
   Choose Your Words Wisely 43
   Be Confident (Not Arrogant) 46
   Be Assertive (When Necessary) 47
   Wherever You Are Physically, Be There Mentally Too 49

KEY 4 – FOCUS on Productivity 53
The Word TRY 53
Each Day Do a Little Bit More 55
You Must Take Action to Get Results 58
Overcome Call Reluctance 59
You Must Have a Plan 62
You Must Have Goals 63
Don't Confuse Activity with Sales Productivity 64
Measure Your Results 67

KEY 5 – PROSPECT Like You are Competing 69
The More You Sell, the More You'll Sell 70
Have a Prospecting Plan 71
Get People to Think Hmmm 73

KEY 6 – RUN Effective Client Meetings 77
Strategize Before Meetings 77
You are a Prospect's Guest 79
Listen and Ask 80
He Who Asks Questions, Manages the Conversation 82
Ask Open Ended Questions 83
Answer a Question with a Question 85
When You Ask Questions, Don't Give Answers ... 87
Pay Less Attention to the Words People Use 89
Presenting Proposals 91
"Thank You" The Positive Ending to a Meeting ... 94

KEY 7 – MANAGE Your Sales Process **95**
   Know the Definition of a Meeting 95
   There are Only 3 Kinds of Meetings 96
   Only 3 Outcomes to Meetings 98
   6 Required Components of Every Sale 99
   A Story about Value 105
   Using a Risk/Benefit Assessment 106
   Think: Let's Do *This* 107
   Level Set Situations 109
   The "Y" Factor 111
   Use Time Wisely with Prospects 115
   Big Foot Hunting / Emotional Selling 116

KEY 8 – BELIEVE You Are Exceptional **119**
   Through Faith and Action, All Things Are Possible 119
   Mistakes and Failures are a Key Part of Success 121
   Competence Leads to Confidence 123
   Manage Your Business to Standards, Not Exceptions 124
   Act, Think and Speak for Where You Expect to Be 126
   Be a Leader 127
   Change Your Sales Culture 128
   Manage Your Life to be an Exception, Not a Standard 131
   Seek to Continually Educate Yourself 133
   If YOU Don't Change, Your Results Won't Change 134

Epilogue **137**

DEDICATION

In 1991, I was involved in a careless automobile accident that should have killed me. God had other plans.
Shortly after that wreck I was on my knees one night praying for help. I needed to find my way out of the bad place that I was in and out of the job I had. Both were not in line with my potential. I prayed for God to bring someone into my life. I needed balance and I just wanted to settle down and marry the right girl.
One month passed.
When I first met Bonnie, I immediately fell in love with her. She wasn't like any other girl that I had ever met. I knew there was something special about her, so I figured that I should probably not let her get away.
One of the many amazing things about her, stood out in something that she said to me shortly after we met, while we were sitting on the steps of my apartment. I told her that I had always felt that I was meant for bigger and better things in life. I told her that I was going to quit my hourly retail job to pursue a corporate sales position.
I said that I needed to do this, so I could step into my potential and improve my life. She smiled at me with that beautiful smile and she said OK.
Bonnie didn't really know me, but she saw something special in me. More importantly she believed in me. In fact, the first

time we met, she told her friend Kristen, "Now that is the kind of guy I could marry." Of course, I was sold on her too.

Five months later on a beautiful Sunday, October 13, 1991, we were married. The wedding was in Bonnie's parent's backyard. It was simple and beautiful.

The very next day, Monday, I started my first corporate sales job in telecom. I was off to a bumpy start as I struggled to learn about a new career and about being a salesman.

A few months later, I would start my second corporate telecom sales job. My confidence was very low.

I nervously packed for the trip to my new hire training, which was being held in Houston, Texas. I arrived at the sales training and opened my suitcase, unsure about my future. Bonnie had placed a piece of paper in my luggage with this scripture: Philippians 4:13: "I can do all things through Christ who strengthens me."

I carried those words on that paper from Bonnie in my pocket the entire week. I would carry those words in my heart the rest of my life.

This story is important for two reasons. First, God can and will answer your prayers in His time and in His way. He understands your situation and He will help you to find a way. It may not always be in the way and timeframe that you like or want, but He will find a way. He always does.

Secondly, when you have someone in your life who believes in you and supports you, you can do just about anything. I am living proof of that.

Bonnie watched me go through failure after failure, to pursue what were now OUR dreams.

Each encounter with failure would bring me closer and closer to success and closer to our dreams.

In 1992, Bonnie's mother, Sharon Malmer, (who always saw the great in me), gave me a Zig Ziglar book. I was introduced to the man with the funny name, who was in the serious business of being successful. My view on sales and myself would change.
My sales style changed and my results improved.
Later my life dream would change to become a motivational speaker. I worked with other telecom companies and after only a few years of being a telecom sales rep, I was promoted to sales manager. I continued my quest for success and became a top producing sales manager. A few short years later, I would be promoted to a Regional Vice President of Sales.
All of this happened with my wonderful and beautiful wife Bonnie standing by me, encouraging me. She has never stopped believing in me and she has never let me stop believing in myself.
Bonnie, my gift from God, is the reason I have never given up.

As of the writing of this book, I am now a Speaker and Sales trainer with the Zig Ziglar Corporation. Tom Ziglar and the Ziglar family also saw something special in me and they helped me to make my life dream a reality.
Thank you Ziglar Family.
To my mother and father, Antonio and Helen Rodriguez, who have always encouraged me and supported me.
To Bonnie's parents, Bill and Sharon Malmer, thank you for the books, the love and the kindness. I miss you Sharon.

The things that happened in this story aren't a coincidence. They never are. God is good.

FOREWORD

Zig Ziglar always said that "Selling is essentially a transference of feeling."

Let's break this quote down into three key concepts:

First, in order to be a successful salesperson you have to be the right kind of person. After all, if you are going to transfer feeling to someone it better start with integrity and trust!

Second, in order to be successful in sales you must absolutely believe 100% that your product or service is exactly what your prospect needs. After all, if you are not convinced that what you are selling is what your prospects need, they won't be either!

Third, in order to be successful in sales you must be a true professional. This means that you hone your skills and internalize everything that your prospect needs to understand about your solution. It means doing the necessary work and having the right attitude during every step of the process. Prospects are smart and the last thing you want to transfer to them is a bad attitude or lack of preparation!

If you agree with these three concepts then I am excited to tell you that you have the right book in your hands!

"8 Keys to Exceptional Selling" not only conveys this message all the way through it and gives you the necessary steps to take, but author Mike Rodriguez lives these three steps every day.

Mike has over 20 years of sales, sales management, and sales training and speaking experience, and I am proud that he is on the Ziglar Corporate Training and Speaking team.

Get out your highlighter and start taking notes as you learn how to take your sales career to the next level!

Tom Ziglar

CEO-Proud Son of Zig Ziglar

8 KEYS TO EXCEPTIONAL SELLING

Thank you to everyone who encouraged me to write this book.

KEY 1

Everything Starts With YOU.

Throughout the world each day, countless salespeople wake up, get dressed and start their morning routine. Some begin at home, while others start the drive to an office.

Once the morning routine is over, the work routine starts. This represents the things you decide to do on a daily basis. These things are inevitably what will decide your end results.

Most of us have the same routine every day.

To a large extent, routine manages all of our lives. This can be good or not, depending on your routines and the outcomes that you are experiencing.

As a salesperson, you should realize that if you want different results, that you must make changes. This book was written for you.

I am a salesperson and I am proud to be in sales. I am passionate about helping people to become their best and I believe that most people want to perform at their best. I also believe that many people just aren't aware of what it takes to reach their potential.

KEY 1 – Everything Starts with YOU.

Then there are those who simply aren't willing to take the action that is required.

At your current employer, you have probably noticed three categories of people:

1. Those who show up because they have to. They do enough just to get by.
2. Those who show up and do the job that the company expects of them.
3. Those who show up to win. They have a winning attitude and they do a little bit more to get the best results.

Which category best describes you? Invest a few minutes and think about your daily routines.

Wherever you think you are today, please know that you can change.
You can be successful in sales and in life, but you must want to. There is also a catch: The best training, sales strategies, and life philosophies will not work, if you won't.

Some show up because they have to.
Most show up and do the work.
Few show up to win.
What's your Decision?

KEY 1 – Everything Starts with YOU.

Throughout my many years of "hands on" sales experience, or as the veterans say, "carrying a bag," I have failed many times. By experiencing these failures I have learned how to win. Through discipline, a strong desire to succeed and a love for sales, I have learned how to craft my skills to a level of high performance. I have practiced the established and proven key strategies in this book over and over again.

You should also understand this, and it will probably disappoint some of you, but here it is: There is not a magical fix to become a top performer. There is not a "silver bullet" or a "magical phrase" that exists, that will allow you to close more sales.
Effective sales results are born from effective salespeople. Effective salespeople become that way by using the tools and resources that are provided to them or that they have decided to find. They continuously train and practice their technique to eventually make it their own. By doing this, they become better each day and they have a direct influence on their own sales results and on their own life.

As you read through this book, you will also learn additional strategies contained within each of the 8 Keys to help you on your journey to success. Your job is to use all of the Keys and strategies contained in this book and to practice them until they become a part of you. You must internalize them.
YOU, my friend, are working to become the best salesperson that you can be, and as a result, you will need to learn effective philosophies and strategies.

My mission is very clear: To help YOU to become exceptional!

KEY 1 – Everything Starts with YOU.

This book was written from a strategic sales perspective. What this means to you is that the Keys and strategies that you will learn are transferable. They can be used in just about any industry or sales job that you are involved with. Why? Because I am going to teach you the 2 secrets that most salespeople overlook: The science of asking questions and the art of listening. But first we need to get YOU straight before we can help others.

You MUST Have a Positive Attitude to Succeed.

You must *believe* to achieve.

Everything starts with your attitude. I consider your Attitude to be the foundation to building a successful you! If your foundation isn't strong, chances are the rest of you will suffer.

Bad attitudes lead to negative thoughts which can break your confidence and create a false sense of fear.

Fear is paralyzing. Fear will then influence your thoughts and in turn, prevent you from taking action!

I have met and worked with many salespeople and I often ask them about their attitude. I'm surprised at the less than positive responses that I get. Considering that we are in a people services industry (yes, that is right...we are serving others), it is critically important to make sure that you give your potential clients the best possible YOU that is available each day!

KEY 1 – Everything Starts with YOU.

Personal ATTIUDE Review:

- How is your attitude every day?
- Are you proud of your profession?
- Do you choose to be positive each day?
- Do you focus on the productive results of sales calls and activities?
- Do you commit yourself to learn each day?
- Do you participate in gossip?
- Do you associate with those who consistently underperform?
- Do you get enough sleep?
- Do you bring personal problems with you to work?
- Do you have a balanced life?

Know this: A positive attitude is a choice. You can choose to be positive each day or you can choose to be negative each day. It truly is your choice.

So why don't you take a few minutes and evaluate your attitude, while I share this:

I remember my first sales job like it was yesterday. I was excited, eager and terrified, all at the same time. I wanted to be successful but I really didn't know how. As a result, I was frustrated, I had a bad attitude, and I set myself up for failure. When my days didn't go well, I would blame the prospect, the weather, the product, my boss, etc.... anything that I could blame to justify my failures. And worse, I was hanging around other negative people who would validate my thoughts and feelings. They would reinforce my negative attitude even more!

KEY 1 – Everything Starts with YOU.

It was only when I decided to change my attitude (and my negative associations) that I started to change my results.

I need to clarify that ***I had*** to change my attitude because I wasn't happy with the results and I realized that I was the only one to blame.

The great news is that if you are negative, somewhere in between, or even positive, it doesn't matter. You can always improve, if you choose to.

Here is how:
Begin by making a decision to change. Then, start investing in YOU and start buying positive books (audio or paper) and read or listen to them daily! Also, be careful and be aware of who and what you are listening to. If you hang around negative people, you will start to become negative. If you hang around complainers, you will start to complain more. And be very aware of lazy people! Zig Ziglar says that people with nothing to do will always want to do it with you!

The point is that you will eventually become like the people that you choose to hang out with. Who can you afford to be around and for how long?

Having a good attitude or a bad attitude truly is a decision and it is your decision every single day of your life. By the way, not making a decision, is in fact, making a decision. It all starts with you. Remember, your attitude is YOUR attitude. You cannot choose some of the things that will happen to you in life, but you can certainly choose what you are going to do about it.

KEY 1 – Everything Starts with YOU.

In sales, a positive attitude is the foundation to success. I call it **The Positive Factor.**

This is when your positive attitude leads to a cycle of increased performance. An initial positive attitude increases your productivity. This leads to more meetings. Those meetings will generate more sales. More sales create performance results: increased skill, awards, commission dollars, recognition, job security, etc. In return, you will improve your attitude!

What do you choose to do?

KEY 1 – Everything Starts with YOU.

You will eventually become like the people you choose to hang around with. Who can you afford to be around and for how long?

When the Pain of Your Current Situation is Greater Than the Pain of Making Change, Then it's Time to Change.

You will encounter many challenges in your life, it is inevitable. You are probably going through some type of difficult time as you read this book. Everyone goes through tough times, but you must know that tough times are always temporary. The way life works is that if you do not have a plan, a positive attitude, and the skillset to improve, you probably will not take action to improve. If you do not take action to improve, then you will not get the results that you desire. Therefore, you will experience some kind of pain in your life.

Pain is relative to each person who is experiencing it, so it is important to come to terms and truly understand the Pain or *Pains* that are in your own life.

Where you are in your life right now is only temporary. It's up to you to let it become permanent.

KEY 1 – Everything Starts with YOU.

An example of a Pain might be that you are struggling with low sales performance, a weight issue, depression, substance abuse, living somewhere you don't like or even working someplace that is not in line with your potential. Pain is any current situation or event in your life that is preventing you from being happy, and that is affecting your quality of life. Pain will take you from the point of seriously considering changing, to the realization that you must take action to change the situation.

If you are not at your ideal weight and your clothes don't fit properly, that might be uncomfortable. However, if you start to experience health issues, the weight issue might now become very painful to you.

The Pain of the current situation, the health issues, now outweighs the Pain of making change, eating right and exercising. As a results, you are now willing to put forth the necessary effort to make the change.

In sales if you aren't performing, you will face repercussions or possible termination, and that is painful. You will have two options:

1. Endure the pain of increased prospecting every day and work to improve, or
2. Endure the pain of looking for, finding, and moving to another job.

By the way, if you choose not to improve, you may get a new job, you may work at a new building with a new logo and be around new people, but just remember this: YOU will still be the same.

You should now get my point.

KEY 1 – Everything Starts with YOU.

If you are experiencing ANY situation that is affecting your quality of life, preventing you from being happy or from becoming the person that you know you need to be, if it is more painful for you to be in THAT situation… then it is time for you to endure the pain of changing.

I had the opportunity to take over a poor performing sales team with the goal to improve their performance. I discovered very quickly that they had adopted extremely negative attitudes and developed less than poor work habits.

I gave a very heartfelt speech to the team and challenged each person to embrace their new beginning with me. I challenged them to rise to their potential. I outlined our new plan for success, which included personal growth & training, skill development, daily planning and goal setting. In addition, I had committed to personally coach each person to succeed if they were just willing to work with me. I asked each of them to go home, make a decision, and come back in the morning to let me know if they were willing to commit to our new plan for success.

Surprisingly, out of 12 people, I only had one person who made the decision to come back and talk with me. He was quite a bit older than the other salespeople. He told me that he was fairly new and had come from another industry. He mentioned that he didn't understand what he was doing and that he was confused about our products.

He also let me know that he was on the final phase of a performance plan. He ended our conversation by saying that he felt like he didn't have any other options but to take a chance on making a change to improve. His feelings were that the plan sounded solid and that he would be willing to work to make it happen.

KEY 1 – Everything Starts with YOU.

He was a great example of a person having enough Pain in his life that he was willing to make a change. His Pain had become greater than the Pain of taking action. He was smart enough to realize this and he made a commitment to improve. He followed my plan everyday with the work ethic, persistence, and consistency of a top performer.

At the end of that year a few things happened for him. First, because he had taken action and sold well over his quota, he was able to get himself removed from his performance plan early on. Next, through his actions and thoughts, he had developed the proper winning mindset. He had indeed become a top performer.

The end result? He joined me on the stage that year to accept his Chairman's Club Award for being one of the top ten salespeople in the company for the year!

Now just think if he had decided not to take action to resolve his Pain. Where would he be and what would have happened? There could have easily been a different and less desirable outcome.

YOU too must evaluate the things in your life that are holding you back and that are preventing you from becoming the person that you want to be. Then, you must decide if it is more painful for you to stay in that situation or if it is more painful for you to take action to change.

KEY 1 – Everything Starts with YOU.

You ALWAYS have a decision,
No matter how difficult or
impossible it may seem.

KEY 1 – Everything Starts with YOU.

You Must Know Your *WHY.*

Your WHY is your purpose. It is not to be confused with a "reason."

If you have a job, most likely the "reason" you have a job is because you need money. So in effect, the REASON that you go to work is to make money. A WHY is much deeper than a reason. A WHY is soul piercing, life impacting and life changing.

If you are having a tough day loaded with refusal and zero sales results, a paycheck might keep you at work, but a purpose, your WHY, will push you to keep on working.

I live in Texas and making outside prospecting calls in the summer with 6 digit temperatures doesn't inspire very many salespeople. In fact, it can be very tempting to give into the career killer called "call reluctance." If you don't have a powerful WHY, it can become very easy to quit prospecting to go and do something else.

When you know your WHY, you start to look at the big picture and you look through the short term Pain of the situation. You understand that Pain is only temporary. You rely on your WHY to inspire you and keep you going.

My WHY is providing the best life for the loves of my life: my beautiful and amazing wife Bonnie and my 5 beautiful, kind and intelligent daughters: Lauren, Lexi, Linsey, Leia and London.

If you don't know what your WHY is, it might take some thought, but it is easy to figure out. Find time to be alone.

KEY 1 – Everything Starts with YOU.

Then think of the Key thing or things in your life that really motivate you, inspire you, and influence you to perform with passion to become and do your very best. The answer will come to you.

Know Your "CORE 4." - Who is Influencing Your Life?

It's Monday morning and you are in the break room at the office getting coffee. Your team members start flowing in and it starts... the gossip and complaints. Complaints about being at work, the complaints about life, etc.

When you are in those situations, you have a decision to make. You can be part of the problem or you can be part of the solution. You must be serious about this part as it can be very career and life impacting.

Most of my life I was under the impression that the people who were nice to me, who supported my bad habits, laughed at my jokes, or just agreed to hang out with me were my friends. I was wrong most of the time.

One day I came to a hard conclusion: The people who were helping me to hold myself down and supporting my negative attitude, probably wouldn't offer to pay my rent or car payment if I lost my job (actually they probably wouldn't have been able to).

It was at this point that I decided to be more aware of who I was letting impact and influence my life and my results!

There is a difference between an acquaintance, a friend, and your Core 4.

KEY 1 – Everything Starts with YOU.

An acquaintance is a person who will usually hang out with you periodically for convenience, and who will also (in most cases) have some kind of a "common interest" with you. It might be school, work, sports, a hobby, a habit, etc. This "interest" is really the only glue that will hold your relationship together.

In contrast, a friend is really interested in the value of your friendship. It goes beyond the common interest and is more personal. A friend is someone who will support you, they will usually be there for you, BUT... most friends will generally agree with you about everything... and that is the problem. It is very difficult to get a true and objective opinion from your friends. Why? They don't want to upset you or disappoint you.

If you are going to improve and become exceptional, you cannot do it with people who are going to agree with you on everything, regardless of how kind they are and what their intentions are. I'm not telling you to ditch your friends. Everyone needs friends. Just be honest and know exactly where you stand with your friends and acquaintances.

I'm telling you that when it comes to making big life changes, you need people in your life who are going to tell you the truth and NOT tell you what you want to hear, however uncomfortable it is for both of you.

This leads us to your Core 4. These are the 4 people who are at the core of your life. You respect them and you look up to and pull something from them. They should be the core influences in your life. More importantly they have your best interest at heart, ALL of the time.

They may tell you things that you may not want to hear, but that you need to hear. Your Core 4 understand your dreams and your goals.

KEY 1 – Everything Starts with YOU.

They may point out the risks associated with those dreams and goals, but they will never discourage you from pursuing those dreams and goals (unless if pursuing them could potentially bring harm to you or others).

Your Core 4 are usually brutally honest. Not with intentions to hurt or criticize you, but because they care about you and want to see you at your best. And finally, your Core 4 will love you unconditionally.

As an example, my Core 4 has grown and now includes my precious wife Bonnie, my parents and Bonnie's parents.

So at this point you should understand how critical it is to evaluate your Core 4. You must evaluate who you are associating with and who is impacting the direction of your life.

This is not negotiable.

Start with however many people you have that qualify to be in your Core 4. You might only have 1 or maybe even none. Be honest and realistic with yourself about who you will allow and who can help you to change and improve your life.

If you don't have anyone who qualifies, start with someone that you respect and trust. Go to them and ask them to mentor you and build up from there.

KEY 1 – Everything Starts with YOU.

- Who are the "Core 4" people that are closest to you?
- How are they impacting your life?
- What kind of person are you when you are around them?
- Do you say or do things you shouldn't when you are around them?
- Do they encourage you and support you when you make decisions to improve or do they laugh at you and/or criticize you?
- Do you become a better person around them?

Evaluate your actions, thoughts, words and behaviors when you are around the people that you hang out with. If your "Core 4" aren't pushing you to be better, then it's time to rethink your Core 4 and start making big changes.

People can either hold you up or hold you down.

Again, I'm not saying to stop talking to people. In fact my directive is quite the opposite. It's YOUR job to bring others up and not to hold THEM down. Find your strength and others will follow.

KEY 1 – Everything Starts with YOU.

Be Genuine and Sincere.

Be yourself, unless you aren't genuine, and in that case work on being genuine. If you follow all of the Keys in this book, you will have no choice but to come across as genuine and sincere. Be honest. If you don't have an answer, don't give a false or half-truth. When selling, take a different approach and respond to your prospect with "that's a great question, I don't have the answer, but I will work to get it." (From a sales strategy perspective, you should then say, "If I am able to get the answer and it solves your concern, are you comfortable with moving forward?")

The end result: If you tell your prospect that you are going to do something for them, then do it. No excuses.

People will like you if you show a genuine interest in them!

Trust, on the other hand, takes time. It is important to do what you say and to respond in a way that makes people feel comfortable. If a prospect isn't ready to buy, but is interested in learning more, then you must schedule a follow-up meeting. You will earn their trust through the time invested in the progression of your meetings together.

If you find yourself being tempted to say something that isn't true, remember that the risk of being exposed for something that isn't true will not only cost you a sale, but will compromise your trust and integrity as well. It simply isn't worth it.

Be aware that some people are leery of sales professionals due to previous negative encounters with unprofessional salespeople.

KEY 1 – Everything Starts with YOU.

In these situations, you have a double challenge to face:

1. They will have built a wall that you must break down, before you get a chance to earn their trust or even get them to like you.

2. You will then need to work on building the trust.

Having a wall built simply means that they will have reservations about opening up to you with any meaningful conversation. This in turn will make it very difficult to make any progress. You must break down the wall first.

You can learn to monitor these types of situations by evaluating their body posture, words & tone and their responsiveness. People with walls simply hide behind them. Be cautious in your approach and give them time to adjust to you. This is not the time for aggressive sales tactics or cheesy one-liners. Respect their position and their concerns. After all you are a guest in their place of business. Engage them by asking questions and then listen.

After time and once they realize you have their best interest at heart, they will break down their walls.

Be Accountable. Don't Blame or Make Excuses.

Has someone ever asked to borrow money from you? It is usually an uncomfortable encounter for both parties. You know what is more uncomfortable? Going to collect from the borrowing party when they don't pay. Why? Because most people who owe you money are not going to be in a position to pay when the time comes. They also probably won't appreciate your follow up call.

KEY 1 – Everything Starts with YOU.

That time when the money is due is called accountability and some people don't like it. Accountability causes some people to go directly into defensive mode. They will deflect the issue back onto the person issuing the accountability. Then they will usually justify their actions with excuses and the ugly sister of excuse: blame.

They might also deflect the matter onto someone or something else.

How does this translate to sales?

When you manage your sales process and run your sales business, it is important that you set the right expectations. If you didn't do your job properly, own it. Then ask the person who you are accountable to what THEY expect as a proper resolution.

This strategy also applies to matters that deal with your prospects, clients and your boss. People do not like excuses and they will not tolerate blame. Neither should you.

I learned at an early age to take accountability for my actions. If you make a mistake, accept responsibility for it, sincerely apologize, and then seek to make resolution. Likewise, be accountable for your successes. Never let someone else steal credit for your successes, but be sure to give enormous credit to those who have helped you.

Your manager, your team and your company depend on you to deliver and to be accountable for your sales numbers. Be honest and forecast accurately. If you are coming up short, let them know and then step up your prospecting and selling skills!

KEY 1 – Everything Starts with YOU.

Know What You Are Selling.

What?!...are you serious Mike? Of course I know what I am selling. But do you?
The average salesperson thinks, and most have internalized, that they must get their products into the hands of the client, whether they need it or not.
Exceptional sales are not made this way. What does it cost you in the long run if you have the wrong mindset?
Here is the wakeup call. You do not sell a product or a service, you sell the result or benefit to the client (not to you) for that service.

If you are selling real estate, you aren't selling homes, you might be selling a better quality of life for a new family or a retiring couple.
Selling Software as a Service? It's not about cost of license per seat, it may be about eliminating the workload from your prospects IT staff, increasing employee productivity and morale. That is priceless!

This is a foundational Ziglar philosophy and one that hit home with me at a low spot in my career. This mindset allowed me to transition from being a hard closer, to becoming a hard listener.
And that is one of the true Keys.

You must listen to your prospects from the time you first meet them, until the time they see the true value from your product or service.

Don't focus on what YOU want or need to sell them, focus on what THEY want or need.

KEY 1 – Everything Starts with YOU.

Dress for SUCCESS! Your Attire is Your Brand, Your Packaging.

For those of you that get this, congratulations! I'm very proud of you. Sales is a very noble profession. In fact, if you are getting paid to sell, then by definition, you are a professional salesperson. As a professional, you must not only BE your best every day, you must also LOOK your best every day.

Let me explain why.

You are your own brand. How you dress is how you will be perceived. It is how you are introducing yourself to the world. Your attire is your packaging! Whether you accept it or not, you are judged by your attire and people will respond to your attire.

No one cares how comfortable you are if you dress sloppy. You will find that your attire has a direct impact on how people view you. Yes you are in sales, so YES you are viewed and judged.

The great news is that you don't have to spend a fortune to look like a true sales pro. But there is another reason that you should always dress professionally: Your client.

Dressing professionally shows that you not only respect yourself, but that you also respect your client. An example I like to use is this:

When you go to a wedding, what do you wear? You wear formal attire. Why? Because the occasion calls for it.

You also dress to show respect for the event, for the people and for yourself.

When you meet with a potential prospect to share the value of your offering, you should dress professionally, because the occasion calls for it.

KEY 1 – Everything Starts with YOU.

In addition, when you dress formal, how do you feel? How do you act? Think about it. You feel like a million dollars and you tend to act more professionally. I'm not asking you to act too formal, but merely to be a professional and to act like a professional. Your prospect deserves it and expects it!

If you are new to sales or just new to the concept of dressing professionally, let me clarify that you dress for "your industry" not for trends.

I have seen corporate salespeople who meet with business clients in polo shirts and khakis. When I ask them why they are dressed that way, they say that the new business trend is business casual. They are wrong. Business casual is only for businesses that allow their employees to dress that way or for industries that have casual wear as a standard. Even then, this almost always does not pertain to salespeople.

It's not about you!

Don't dress for how you feel or want to feel.

For those of you that aren't sure about your attire, I'm going to cover the basics to make sure that we are on the same page. If you already dress like a professional daily, you can simply use this as reinforcement.

KEY 1 – Everything Starts with YOU.

A standard sales attire summary:

- A suit - tie is always optional depending on the industry. You can go to a discount store and get a nice 100% wool suit for about 50%off of retail prices. For women it is comparable.
- Shoes – Business style that are clean. For women: no open toes and no sandals. For men: invest in a nice pair of dress shoes, black, brown or dark burgundy is the easiest.
- Shirt – Men: color isn't an issue (I prefer white or blue). Look sharp but not too trendy. You may think you are fashionable, but the executive you are meeting with may see you differently. Women: conservative is always best.
- Always make sure your clothes are wrinkle free.
- Make sure that you are clean and kept, with brushed hair and fresh breath!
- Wear a smile and be warm and inviting!
- People will respond to the signals that you send out.
- Project professionalism and respect and it will be returned.

Have Integrity. Enough said.

The basis of integrity is really doing what you say you are going to do and doing the right things consistently.
Have integrity always and in everything that you do. It's easy to lose and it's almost impossible to gain back when you have lost it. Having integrity means having moral principles, honesty, ethics, honor and sincerity.

KEY 1 – Everything Starts with YOU.

KEY 1 SUMMARY

❖ How is your attitude? Would others agree?
❖ What are the pains that you are experiencing in your life that you need to take action to change?
❖ What is your WHY?
❖ Who are you CORE 4?
❖ How are you presenting YOU as a brand?

KEY 2 – EMBRACE the Art & Science of Sales

KEY 2

EMBRACE the Art & Science of Sales

When I conduct a sales training, I reference these two words: Art and Science, and I usually get mixed responses from salespeople. Why? Because everyone has a different definition of sales. Some people even question me as to how or why sales can even be placed in either category.

Here is how and why: Through my two decades plus of working in sales, I have run thousands of prospecting calls, attended a few thousand live meetings and closed millions of dollars of revenue. I have worked with people and businesses of all types and sizes and I have learned a few things: You must know your numbers, metrics and planning (the Science) and you must master your selling skills, strategy and personal development (the Art).

When you are focused on these areas, you become more efficient. When you become more efficient you sell more, when you sell more you help other people and when you help other people you will attain your goals.

KEY 2 – EMBRACE the Art & Science of Sales

The Art of Sales

Selling and communicating is an art. Art requires skill and skill is developed through practice. It is the correct usage of the right words and crafting your words in a way that makes sense to your prospect. It is the use of your eyes to stay focused on your prospects. Not in an evasive or creepy way, but to maintain proper attention. Your posture, your hands & facial expressions convey your feelings and your interest in your prospect. They also reveal your confidence level. You must communicate properly and most importantly, you must listen, listen and listen! Excluding prospecting, this is actually probably the hardest part of sales.

The Art of sales is basically HOW you communicate when you sell and WHO you are as a salesperson.

Ironically one of the ways you learn how to sell is from selling the wrong way. You can also learn from those who have consistently been successful selling throughout their career. Developing your sales art encompasses these two areas:

1. Learning through listening, and
2. Modifying your behavior and words, so you can provide the best solutions for your prospect.

Art is mastered through practice and therefore you must continually practice if you want to master the art of sales. When and how do you practice sales? Anytime you have a chance to interact with other people.

You develop your art every time you listen to the words someone uses and you understand what they are telling you.

KEY 2 – EMBRACE the Art & Science of Sales

You develop your art every time you talk with someone and help them to understand what you are saying by using your words to paint a descriptive picture in their mind.

You develop your art when you sit up in your chair and focus on your prospect. You keep your body facing towards them, your eyes on their eyes and your thoughts and ears on their words.

If you are thinking about what you are going to say next, you cannot effectively listen to your prospect. They will pick up on this very quickly and any trust you have established will be lost just as quickly. The art of sales is also using words in a way, NOT to manipulate, but to generate an understanding.

I call this the HMMM factor. (We will cover this later, but it is basically prompting people to respond with a "Hmmm" in agreement with what you just shared.) The HMMM factor means that you must communicate in a way that actually makes sense to them.

The art of sales is the effective use of your words and actions, to convey solutions or to respond to a prospect through effective listening to their words.

KEY 2 – EMBRACE the Art & Science of Sales

The Science of Sales

Don't let this part scare you. It is critical and it is also fun.

Most salespeople think of science (the How) and metrics (the Numbers) as the manager's job. Then, unfortunately, they sometimes categorize it as "micro-management" when the manager asks them about their numbers, strategy and activity. That kind of thinking is ridiculous and irresponsible and will inevitably lead to less than desirable sales results.

The reality is this: managing your metrics is YOUR responsibility. Yes you heard correctly, it is your job to prospect and manage your results and your own deficiencies. You must also track your own progress.

If you bought this book on your own, I would suspect that you are capable of making your own decisions, so please apply decision making skills to ALL aspects of your life, including your career.

So what exactly are Metrics?

Metrics are your numbers.
Metrics includes things like Time Management segments, such as scheduling time each day to prospect with start and stop times. If you have a set time to prospect each day, you can then manage the number of prospecting calls that you are making during those set times.

This allows you to monitor your progress and to be aware of potential issues you might have with call reluctance or again with skill deficiencies.

KEY 2 – EMBRACE the Art & Science of Sales

For example if you have scheduled yourself to start prospecting at 1:30 and to call until 3:30, you would manage the following:

- Did I start at the time I committed? If not, maybe you have call reluctance or lack of discipline to initiate your plan.
- Did I make adequate calls for a 2 hour session? If you are telemarketing and you average 1 "dial" a minute, and you DO NOT talk with any decision makers, you should have made 60 dials per hour or up to 120 dials for the session. If not, figure out why you aren't making enough dials. Again, maybe call reluctance is the issue or maybe an increase in your tempo (dial faster) or maybe you have a lack of prospects to call on.
- How many decision makers did I talk to? Keep track of the time it takes you to have a conversation with a decision maker. I'm not saying to rush a conversation, I'm asking you to really keep track of the time that you spend talking to a decision maker versus that actual time that it should take (on average), to talk with a decision maker.
- How many NEW meetings did I set? This number will be a direct result of how many decision makers that you spoke with and in turn will give you your "prospecting" closing ratio (Not to be confused with your SALES closing ratio).
- Did I call until the end time that I committed to? If not, maybe you experienced call reluctance, maybe you didn't have enough prospects to call on or maybe you just reached your goal early and decided to cool your jets.

KEY 2 – EMBRACE the Art & Science of Sales

- Did I attain my goals? This one is easy if you are managing all of these metrics. If you have goals, you can then measure yourself against your success in attaining your goals.

Managing your metrics this way will give you a basic foundation that you can apply to your prospecting sessions.

In addition, the science of sales means that you track and know these additional crucial metrics:

- Average dials/cold calls to Decision Makers (DM) I actually reached
- DM's I spoke with versus new meetings set after talking to those DMs
- New meetings set vs. meetings actually attended. This allows you to check the quality of your meetings. If most of your meetings cancel, evaluate what you are saying.
- Meetings that have progressed to proposals
- Proposals presented vs. meetings closed
- Meetings closed vs. meetings attended
- Your actual Closing Ratio

So now you should be able to see that your metrics really are your responsibility and that they are critically important!

The science of sales also includes strategizing on client meetings and opportunities, knowing your industry and go to market strategies and learning from different people and sales situations that you encounter. You must also read books, attend trainings and find a quality mentor to continue your sales education.

KEY 2 – EMBRACE the Art & Science of Sales

You should have a new understanding that managing your metrics and knowing your sales science will allow you to manage your results. This will allow you to identify and point out deficiencies and strong areas that you need to be aware of to improve and to reach your goals.

You must know your numbers.

If you don't know your numbers, how do you know when to start, where to start and where to go? You need to know what to accomplish and if you are doing enough to get the right results.

KEY 2 SUMMARY

- ❖ What are you doing each day to improve your sales techniques?
- ❖ How are you managing your own metrics?
- ❖ What are your main areas of improvement?
- ❖ How are you preparing for your next one-on-one / review of your performance?
- ❖ How can you improve your performance?

KEY 3

THINK About Your Prospect.

Let's talk MINDSET real quick: A poor salesman thinks he is doing something TO someone. According to Ziglar: Sales isn't something that you do TO someone, Sales is something that you do WITH or FOR someone.

Every salesperson would be better off and all would experience a greater level of success if they would follow this philosophy.

On every sales call that I've been on someone gets sold,

The prospect: who gets a new solution, or

The salesperson: who gets to move on to the next prospect.

I have learned the hard way, through my many years of business meetings, that it is never about you. It is always about the prospect. Therefore, you must genuinely be in tune with your prospect's needs. You must never be focused on getting a sale or making commissions.

That's not to say that getting a sale isn't important. It is. So are commissions. But they will probably never happen if that is all you are thinking about.

KEY 3 – THINK About Your Prospect

I'm talking about purpose-filled direction and planning, by going into a meeting and telling yourself that you will take notes and listen. That you have convinced yourself that you are there to find a solution. That you will not talk to the prospect with dollar signs in your eyes. People can tell if you are there for you or if you genuinely want to help them.

This means if you are a talker, stop talking. Your client cannot talk if you are talking and therefore you cannot hear what they need to tell you.

Are you happy and do you carry a smile? Look in a mirror or ask someone to evaluate your facial expressions and your eye contact when you present or role play.

People also respond to us based on the way that we present ourselves. If we show up and we are too casual or act in a manner that is unprofessional, they might not respond positively. Also, if we act too formal and present our product and service as complicated, they will respond accordingly.

Here is a story about this for those of you who have kids or who have nieces or nephews or who have ever seen a child.

If a small child runs, trips and falls down what do they do? They immediately look up at the adult who is with them and watching them, so they can determine what their response will be to the situation:

If that child falls down, looks up and the parent is screaming and crying, the child will start screaming and crying. If the child looks up and the parent says "Oh my, you had a fall, but you are ok," the child will smile and go on their way. Why? It's the way we were made. We respond to our surroundings and the people that we are with.

KEY 3 – THINK About Your Prospect

This philosophy also applies in sales situations. If you are presenting a product in a complex way, people will respond that way, and as a result, they will want time to "think about it." They will feel it is a complex decision that requires more thought.

Throughout my journeys, I have determined that we learn from people through a 3 step process:

1) By asking the right kinds of questions.

2) By carefully listening to their response and understanding the meaning behind their words.

3) By choosing how we respond to what we have just heard.

KEY 3 – THINK About Your Prospect

Never Negotiate with Fear or Mediocrity.

If you negotiate with fear you will lose. You must also know that Doubt and Uncertainty are the appetizers of fear. Your mind feeds off of them until you become full of fear. If you allow fear to enter your thoughts, the thing that you fear will grow until it eventually owns your thoughts. Once your thoughts are owned, your actions are owned.

Fear is paralyzing.

Fear is probably the number 1 killer of dreams. Why? Because fear prevents action!

Regarding mediocrity, it is like a vacuum. It sucks you in and holds you there.

Get my point about fear and mediocrity? This is serious business!

Doubt and Uncertainty are the appetizers of fear. Your mind feeds off of them until you become full of fear.

KEY 3 – THINK About Your Prospect

Now here is the great news: You do not have to accept fear. It is your choice. Look at it this way: Fear is actually your very own brain, hyper thinking about the things that you are worrying about and creating potential situations and their possible outcomes, all of which usually NEVER HAPPEN! That's right. Studies have shown that most things that we are afraid of or worry about never happen.

Franklin D. Roosevelt (FDR) said, "The only thing we have to fear is fear itself." When I was younger I didn't understand this quote and would say things to myself like, "Well he doesn't know my situation." I can tell you from personal experience that probably 99.99% of the things that I have worried about in my life have never come true.

When it comes to sales, it's easy to doubt yourself and your abilities. It's easy to fear cold calling, fear rejection, a big sales call or maybe even making a presentation. You might even fear success.

You must get to the point that you choose to think positive and healthy thoughts. Thoughts that are empowering. The kind that drive your mind to act and to do. Thoughts that remind you of your goals, your purpose and your passions. You must think of the end result and you must visualize your own success. You must believe in yourself and face the thing or things that you fear the most.

As you face your fears, you will defeat your fears.

Your fears then strengthen you and you become stronger and more confident. Fear can be paralyzing or fear can be controlled.

You can and must overcome your fears to help you become a better you and an exceptional salesperson.

KEY 3 – THINK About Your Prospect

Knowledge and Strategies Must be Internalized.

You aren't a robot so don't act like one.

Let's pause for a minute and consider this. Confidence comes from "knowing" what you know. Right? Well if that is true, then we must conclude that we "Know" what we know, by internalizing what we have learned. Does that make sense? Of course it does.

To memorize means to recall to memory.

To internalize your sales process, sales pitch and sales strategy does not mean memorizing it.

This means it actually becomes part of you. A part of your vocabulary and a part of your mindset, so your words flow and sound natural. If you have ever had a telemarketer call you on the weekend with a memorized script, you know exactly what I mean. Ask that telemarketer a question and you will hear silence on the phone. Why? Because they have not internalized their script. The script is doing the thinking for them.

A story about internalizing.

It was the month of January into the New Year. I was in the sales office reminiscing over the previous year and all of the challenges and successes that we faced. I was amazed and very proud of my sales team who had finished the Number 1 team in the company, with 4 Salespeople in the top 10 and I was ranked the number 1 manager.

We had consistently achieved a great level of success every month throughout the previous year and had consistently beaten every sales team, about 44 teams, 11 months out of the previous year (we came in 2nd one month). I had also received a

KEY 3 – THINK About Your Prospect

Chairman's Club Award and a Manager of the Year Award. I heard a knock on my office door and looked up to see our sales trainer. She greeted me and walked in and proceeded to ask if I would be willing to attend the new hire training the next morning as a guest speaker, to deliver a speech on "the secret to success." Wow, what a cool thing to do and what a great honor. I love to speak and help others and I love sales, so marry them all and it was a done deal! Of course I was going to do it, but I told her there was a catch. I gently stated that there really wasn't a secret to success. She looked at me curiously and said, well you know what I mean. I said ok, but assured her that the salespeople might be surprised by my presentation, she just smiled, turned and walked away.

WHERE IS YOUR SCRIPT!?

The next morning I arrived at the hotel conference room for the new hire training and was promptly and warmly greeted by the trainer. She informed me that everyone was really looking forward to hearing the speech of the top performing sales leader in the entire company. I was humbled and calm. She looked down at my empty hands and anxiously exclaimed "Where is your script!?" I calmly looked back at her and gave a slight shrug with my hands open and said, "I don't have one. But don't worry, I don't need one." She quickly responded, "What do you mean? What will you cover? How will you know what to say?" Again, I responded confidently assuring her that I had things under control.

You see, I knew something that she didn't: When you do something well, you internalize it. When you internalize it, you know it. When you know it, you can confidently share it.

KEY 3 – THINK About Your Prospect

You see I knew exactly what I was going to say, because I had personally lived, talked and breathed every day, for many years, the examples and strategies that I was going to share. I had made it an art... My Art.

My thoughts had become my actions and my actions had become my habits. Talking about what made me successful was about as easy as asking an Italian chef to share how he or she makes a great lasagna!

So, I was escorted into the large conference room where I introduced myself and I gave a powerful and sincere speech on becoming successful. (Which by the way was primarily the principles found in this book).

If you want to know how my "secret of success" speech went, it was something like this (condensed version): Have a great attitude, plan your day, know your stuff, practice, read, train, listen to your clients, execute your plan, never give up and repeat daily. The speech was received well with very positive feedback from the group. However, at the end of the speech I personally learned two lessons:

1. Make sure you know your stuff (I did), and

2. Make sure your speech has a format (mine didn't).

A format creates direction and makes the ride smooth for everyone. So that is how you become better. You make mistakes, learn and become better.

KEY 3 – THINK About Your Prospect

Choose Your Words Wisely.

As a mentor, I often train my students on properly selecting and using words. An example that I often use is this: Think back to high school. If your teacher said to you:

1. "I need you to stay after school because there is something that I need to **"discuss"** with you."

What would you think she wants? The common response that I get is that most people believe that they would be in some kind of trouble.

Now if I change only one word... the word "discuss" and change it to "share"... consider the effects again:

2. "I need you to stay after school because there is something that I need to **"share"** with you."

Ok... NOW what would you think that your teacher wants? In this case, the common response that I get is that the same people now believe that there is something "good" that is going to happen. Remember only one word was changed, but the entire meaning of the sentence was changed according to the person receiving the words.

This should validate to you the value, importance and the impact of the words that you choose. You must always ensure that you are using the proper words. Make sense? Good. So how does this translate to sales? Never use vague words like try, hope, maybe, think, kinda or I'll see. These words are noncommittal and compromise confidence!

Instead use confident and forward thinking words like: we will, we can, we will work to and we plan to. Select words like: we, our and your instead of "I" when talking with your prospects.

KEY 3 – THINK About Your Prospect

These words take the focus off of YOU and place it where it should be…on your prospect! Don't say I'd like to, I'd love to or I was hoping to. They are self-centered and ineffective. Here is an example of a standard sales approach used in the marketplace today:

A) I would just love to take some of your time to see if I can help you by presenting my fantastic product.

Here is a better version. Make note of which words have been added, omitted or changed.

B) If you would be willing to invest 15 minutes, I can share with you how our product has been helping businesses just like yours. Is that fair?

Example A) lacks confidence and is salesperson focused. Example B) in contrast, is strategically worded. It is confident, implies investment and return, it is sharing and is customer focused.

I will caution you to make sure that you only use words that you would typically use in a common conversation, that are comfortable and flowing to your vocabulary. For example, use "Does that make sense?" instead of saying, "Can you see the value in exploring this as an option to implement your existing infrastructure?" Your prospect needs to relate to you and understand you.

Focus on positive words that allow your prospect to agree. Use "share" instead of "discuss, present or review."

"Let me share this with you" is received better by your prospect than "Let me discuss this" or "Let me present this."

KEY 3 – THINK About Your Prospect

Here are the facts: Nobody wants to *discuss* anything with you nor do they want you to *present* anything to them or *review* anything with you.

Instead of saying "I wanted to see if..." say "I need to share with you how..." These words are "forward thinking" and transfer a feeling of confidence!

When you become aware of the words that are coming out of your mouth, you then become aware of your thoughts and in turn you think about the right words to use.

Using the right words also applies to staying away from your industry terminology and acronyms when talking with your prospect.

Communicating effectively means using words so that you can be understood. If you are using words relative to your industry, your prospect may not understand you and as a result they can become disconnected. It takes practice, so use positive words centered on others in your personal life, as well as in all of your conversations.

Being an effective communicator takes practice. It is a full time job, because you are communicating all of the time!

KEY 3 – THINK About Your Prospect

Be Confident! (Not Arrogant).

People associate with and buy from people who they like and trust.

There is a way to get people to like and trust you, but it will only happen when they decide. Be friendly, honest and genuine and have integrity. People want to buy from someone who knows what they are talking about. Someone who has their best interest at heart. Even if you don't have the answer, if you can confidently respond by saying, "That is a great question, however I don't have the answer right now, but I will get it for you," is received better than saying, "Oh Boy! I really don't know" or "I'm pretty sure." These lack confidence and will probably prevent your prospect from becoming your client. (Never lie...ever! There is never a situation that you should ever lie.)

Liking someone is complicated and can and will vary per individual. There are key things that you can practice to improve the likelihood that someone new will like you. In fact, you already possess the tools and skills necessary.

BE Likeable!

A genuine smile is universal and is contagious! I have been to many businesses and stores and encountered salespeople who have greeted me insincerely. Example "HEY BUDDY!" The fact is, it turns people off and a wall will be built with your prospect before you even get a chance to get them to warm up to you. Be considerate and respectful of your prospects time and of their environment.

KEY 3 – THINK About Your Prospect

When I am a few minutes late to a client meeting, I always genuinely apologize and it is received well. Remember you are a guest of your prospect, so act like one! If someone offers you a water, coffee or soda, take it! Why? It's the first gesture of giving and it allows you to receive something from them. (It also allows you to stay there a little longer.)

Genuine confidence is a sign that you love what you are doing, that you know what you are doing and that you are capable. People trust confidence, but they can also sense phony, so be sincere. Arrogance conveys that you are all about you. Confident people provide solutions and handle situations with care and assertiveness. Arrogant people are all about "me, me, me," not about the prospect or anyone else for that matter.

Contain your ego, your pride and your self-importance. If you are not sure if you are arrogant, ask someone in your Core 4.

Be Assertive (When Necessary).

Judge Ziglar was the brother of Zig Ziglar. He wrote a book called "Timid Salespeople Have Skinny Kids."

It's always interesting to see the number of salespeople who are afraid to ask prospects direct questions, especially when the questions are specifically about helping the prospect. This isn't about interrogating someone; it's about asking sales questions like:

"Are you comfortable with the solution that we are proposing?" or

KEY 3 – THINK About Your Prospect

"Do you see how this will provide a solution to fit your needs?"

You MUST get to the point where you are comfortable asking these types of questions. After all, you are in sales!

This also isn't about being pushy. A pushy salesperson is usually that way for 2 reasons:

1. Because the salesperson is not at quota and is relying on this one deal, or

2. Because the prospect doesn't see any value and the salesperson is pushing to convince the prospect to buy.

Let me also explain the difference between being Assertive and Aggressive.

Being Aggressive is approaching someone in a confrontational manner, either verbally or physically, with self-intentions and with a complete disregard to their boundaries.

In contrast, according to Wikipedia:
Assertiveness is being confident with boundaries and without being aggressive.

Let me make this clear. Under no circumstances should you ever be aggressive or pushy.

I'll remind you again that sales isn't doing something to someone, it's doing something for or with someone. An assertive salesperson is confident in their product and in their solution; therefore they don't need to be aggressive.

KEY 3 – THINK About Your Prospect

Wherever You Are Physically, Be There Mentally Too.

This is part of the discipline of sales that falls under the category of the art of sales. I'm going to tell a story to share an example:

When I was a senior in high school, a group of friends invited me to attend a day of celebration for the traditional senior skip day. I was really excited about going and immediately committed to go. Shortly afterwards, our principal directly announced at a school assembly that the school frowned upon the senior skip day. Furthermore, he stated that anyone who participated in the senior skip day would face repercussions that involved serious punishment.

This was now a game changer for me, because not only did I not want to get in trouble at school, but my father was also a heavy disciplinarian. After a very brief and emotionally based ineffective decision making process, I reluctantly decided to go.

The day arrived and I nervously went with my friends, blatantly skipping school, without permission from my parents or my school.

A large group of us drove to a beautiful area in the mountains that day. People were swimming, cooking out, playing music, throwing Frisbee and having a great time. Everyone brought something and everyone was extremely happy and having a bunch of fun. Everyone that is, except for me.

I was so worried about getting in trouble and so nervous about the events that might transpire the next day, that I was literally incapable of engaging my mind to be happy or even to participate in any of the fun! I was there physically, but not mentally.

KEY 3 – THINK About Your Prospect

The end result. I did indeed get in trouble. So did most of my friends. But here is the big difference:

They HAD fun... I Didn't.

I had paid the price by getting in trouble with absolutely no benefit.

I was there physically, but not mentally.

(I need to clarify that I'm not saying to be happy when doing something wrong, I'm merely using the example of "being there" mentally wherever you are).

I carried this lesson with me throughout most of my life and committed to learn from it.

This is tough because "being where you are" requires preplanning, commitment and mental discipline. In business and in sales, we face this type of mental struggle daily, sometimes from the start of getting out of bed.

For me personally, I used to start thinking and worrying about work first thing in the morning, overlooking the valuable time with my family. I would rush through the morning events to get in the car and eagerly start the drive to the office.

Once in the car I was thinking about other things instead of using my drive time wisely. Then after time passed at the office, my mind would start drifting back to home, regretting the time that I overlooked with my family and thinking about the evening. Once I got home, this mental process of regret would start in reverse, with me thinking of work.

KEY 3 – THINK About Your Prospect

KEY 3 SUMMARY

- ❖ Are you physically and mentally where you are when you are with someone?
- ❖ When you are making cold calls is your mind strategizing and focusing on your goals and results?
- ❖ When you are in meetings are you taking notes or are you thinking of something else?
- ❖ When you are with your spouse, friend or client, do you give them your full attention or is your mind somewhere else?

KEY 3 – THINK About Your Prospect

Give others the respect that they deserve when they are with you. They will appreciate it and in return they will give more back to you.

KEY 4

FOCUS On Productivity

Eliminate the Word TRY From Your Vocabulary.

This will be difficult for some of you to understand but you must know that the word TRY in essence, doesn't exist. I'll prove it. Find a pen or pencil right now (you can use a marker too) and go stand next to a table (with this book). Go ahead I'll wait...

OK, you are back. Now here is our experiment to offer proof:

A. Set the pen or pencil down on the table.
B. Now "TRY" to pick it up.
C. ONLY TWO (2) things just happened:

1. It is OFF of the table, and you are holding it in your fingers. You "DID" successfully pick it up.
2. It is still ON the table, but you are touching it with some degree of pretending to pick it up or touching it and acting like you are straining. In this case, you in fact "DID NOT" pick it up.

KEY 4 – FOCUS On Productivity

See, there is proof. You either PICK the pen up, or you DO NOT pick the pen up. Such is life. You either DO something, or you DO NOT do something.

"TRY" is a conditional yes or no, with the option of an "out". The word TRY is merely an excuse that a person gives you to prepare you for the NO that they will offer when things get too tough or if they decide to quit or not even do it at all.

Don't TRY to do things. Do them or don't do them. When you commit to something and you actually say that you "will do it" or that you "won't do it," an amazing thing happens. When you commit "to do" something, your mind starts thinking of ways to get to the end results, without the option of quitting. Your mind practically eliminates excuses. When you commit "not to do" something it is liberating! You have just become honest and saved yourself and the other person heartache!

I work hard at not using the word TRY. I teach people to work at removing it from their vocabulary and instead focus on giving committal answers.

I was giving the TRY speech to a group of new hire salespeople and a gentleman raised his hand and said to me "that is not true about the word TRY." I asked him to elaborate. He went on to say "Well I tried out for college baseball one time." I asked him if he made the team. He said no. I said this to him. You did not TRY. You actually **did it**... ***you went out*** and auditioned for the team. But you did not make it. Your action resulted in a failure. Which is ok. You see sometimes you do things and succeed and sometimes you do them and you fail.

We have learned to use the word TRY in our society as a justification and acceptance for failure. How many times have you heard this: "Well, at least he tried!" We have conditioned ourselves to say phrases like this, because we view failure as

KEY 4 – FOCUS On Productivity

negative or as a personal defect. We must change our thinking. If you TRY to do something, you are already going into it with the wrong mindset and without a full commitment.

You are already setting yourself up for failure. You must commit and find a way to get it done. You might fail and fail over again, but that is when you get back up and keep DOING it!

When you stand with your potential husband or wife to get married, you are asked if you commit to take this person for better or worse. Nobody says, "I'LL TRY!" You commit and find a way to get it done! You get the point?

Each Day Do a Little Bit More and You Will Become a Little Bit Better."

I have practiced this most of my sales career and I have been able to experience turning many of my personal failures into small successes by changing my daily habits. These good habits will lead to small successes. Those small successes have eventually led me to bigger and bigger successes while on my life's journey.

The reason that statement is so important is this: It is the little things that you "do" or "do not do" each day that will determine your own level of success. The little things do add up! These small things then become bigger things, or even smaller things, depending on which path you choose to follow. For example, if you short yourself 10 prospecting calls a day, you will then lose 50 calls a week which then equates to 200 lost calls per month!

KEY 4 – FOCUS On Productivity

When you translate that into prospects, closing ratios and the value of each sale for your industry, you can see precisely what I mean!

You have to get your mindset right about who you are, where you are going and what you choose to do.

I also see many salespeople that are looking for the proverbial BIG DEAL (Whales/Elephants)! They miss their call targets each week because in their mind, they do not need to make them. It inevitably costs them, mentally and revenue wise, every month they don't close that big deal. You know who they are. They are the "I only work Big Deals" people... and you might even be one. The challenge with this is simple.
It is not a strategy.

BIG DEAL hunting is an emotional based mindset that is fueled by dreams and sustained by complacency. It is the justification that as long as I believe that it is coming in, then I have the right to wait on it. Well, you don't. As long as you collect a salary from your employer, you have a responsibility to continually prospect and perform. Big deal hunting only works if you consistently bring one in every quota measurement period.

There are several other factors that can and will impact your success (shared throughout this book) however your willingness to do a little more and become a little better each day is critical.

You don't gain 30 extra pounds over night. As you increase your caloric intake each day you will gradually, over a period of time, increase your weight. If you decrease your caloric intake each day, over a period of time, you will decrease your weight.

KEY 4 – FOCUS On Productivity

The same applies to your sales career, so you must have a daily plan that keeps you on track to become better. Make sense? Good. Now what does this have to do with sales? Everything!

Several years ago I was speaking at a new hire sales training for a large group of aspiring salespeople. Afterwards, I was eagerly approached by one of the new hires. He thanked me for the wonderful sales information and then he said something that was startling to me:
"You are a really great salesman, I'd bet you could sell ice cubes to Eskimos." I understand that he was complimenting me, however, I immediately responded to him by saying that I would need to apologize to him. He replied by asking what I meant. I elaborated by saying, "What value would Eskimos have in buying ice cubes from me?"
He seemed confused.

So please get the point again: sales isn't something that you do to someone, it is something that you do FOR someone.

You do this by being the best that you can be. By teaching yourself to have integrity, passion, focus, knowledge and patience, so you can benefit your prospects and in return change your own life.

So how do you start to become an "Exceptional Salesperson?" Well, you simply start by making a decision to be Exceptional. You work on changing you and your thinking, so you can believe that you are a problem solver and a solution provider!

KEY 4 – FOCUS On Productivity

You Must Take Action to Get Results.

Most people should have goals and dreams. A dream to change something in their life, a goal to become better or a desire to do something or accomplish something.

However, another primary issue that prevents success, in addition to lack of planning, is a failure to execute!
You must take some kind of action to get your plan in motion. If you want to lose weight, start by ordering healthy food choices, the very next time you eat! Want to get in shape? Start by taking a walk... today! Want to be number one on your team, make the decision and start your new plan today!
This is called taking the first step.
When you take the first step, you have taken action. Action is the necessary component for anyone to start doing anything.

When I look back on my life and recall the times that I needed to improve, every single situation required the exact same thing: ACTION.

When my sales were down, I needed to prospect more. When I needed to lose weight, I needed to eat less and exercise more. When I was feeling low, yep you guessed it, I needed to get up and go forth and sell!

You must learn to take action in any endeavor that you are faced with. Taking action ensures *"some kind of result."* Taking action with direction, leads to measurable progress. Repeating actions after encountering failure, strengthens your ability to keep going.

KEY 4 – FOCUS On Productivity

Taking action means that you don't give in to all of the excuses and fears that your mind will present to you and even justify to you! When you choose to take action, you develop new habits that allow you to continue to stay consistent. Being consistent while being persistent does a few things for you.

1. It allows you to overcome fear and procrastination

2. It allows you to create new habits

3. It validates that you are strong and keeps you going

4. You recognize that encountering failure is a critical part of the journey to success.

And last but not least,

5. You become more confident and better prepared when you face obstacles like how to...

OVERCOME CALL RELUCTANCE!

Call Reluctance is real.

It is a real disease (not medically speaking of course) of salespeople (and people in general) and it kills many sales careers and prevents exceptional selling!

Call Reluctance is different for each person, but similar in this way: (My Definition)- It is the emotional logic that we use, consciously or subconsciously to engage in any activity, other than sales/productive activity, that directly or indirectly prevents us from engaging in productive sales prospecting activity.

KEY 4 – FOCUS On Productivity

Call reluctance can be blatant: "I really don't want to make prospecting calls right now" or it can be more subtle: "I am aware that I need to prospect right now, but I really need to call my wife and see if she found my lost sock instead."

Most salespeople that I have worked with have (or have had) call reluctance to some degree. Personally, I have witnessed call reluctance with friends and family members who are not in sales, who had to make phone calls for business purposes.
I certainly have experienced it and I have found that the only way to battle call reluctance mentally is to acknowledge it, have a positive & confident attitude, create a detailed plan for prospecting and actually start prospecting.

A positive attitude backed by a solid plan, guides your success and can prevent or minimize your failures.

Be confident that good things will happen and make proper plans for your prospecting. By doing this, chances are stronger that you WILL make your calls. This is a better option instead of convincing yourself NOT to make your calls.

I know and have trained many salespeople who have taken drastic measures daily to battle their call reluctance. When I say battle, what I mean is that they are fighting a battle each day to create new habits that promote discipline and action; therefore reducing or eliminating their call reluctance.

KEY 4 – FOCUS On Productivity

A few good measures to counter call reluctance:

1. Set daily goals.
2. Set calendar reminder/meetings with yourself for prospecting.
3. Hang out with people that want to be successful. Go prospecting and on sales calls with a top producer, until you can develop the right discipline and confidence to go on your own.
4. Have a call competition with a peer, as an accountability measure to ensure that you make your calls.

Earlier in my sales career while working in outside sales, I found that more often than not, I would give in to call reluctance and end up going home. I knew this was detrimental to my career, but the fear to cold call and face rejection was overwhelming, so I came up with a plan.

When I would start my drive home, I would allow myself to keep going, as long as I would pull over and cold call at businesses along the way. I would do this every day and eventually over a period of time I had created a habit. Amazingly, not even aware of this, I had created a cold calling habit AND I had minimized my fear of cold calling.

Figure out what your plan is and start your plan today.
DO NOT procrastinate!

Procrastination is the master symptom of call reluctance.

KEY 4 – FOCUS On Productivity

You Must Have a Plan.

A plan is your specific action with dates and tasks that you have assigned to yourself or someone else to guide you in attaining your goals. A plan helps you measure and track your progress to identify your shortfalls and ensures your success. It is your roadmap.

For example, if your goal is to buy a new car, after you have determined the exact car that you want, your plan might include:

- The purchase date
- The purchase price
- Amount you might need to save each month
- Dealerships that you will shop to get your car

If you invest time in making a plan, this will validate that your target or goal will indeed be real to you.

You will find that the more passionate you are about a goal, the more time you will spend thinking about it and the more action you will take. Take time to think about ways that you can plan each day in your sales career.

So now you know what a plan is, but what about your plan to get to your goal?

KEY 4 – FOCUS On Productivity

You Must Have Goals.

A goal is your target that you will attain. If you don't have targets in your life, how will you know where to go and what to shoot for? Goals are the reality of your plan to succeed. Most of us have heard about goals but we don't really know what a goal is. You will learn right now.

A goal must have all of these components in order to be considered a goal: CHECK LIST
- ✓ It must be specific
- ✓ It must be measurable
- ✓ It must be realistic
- ✓ It must be something that you truly want.
- ✓ It must have a specific target/end date

This is NOT A "GOAL" example: "I would like go on vacation sometime next year."

This is NOT A "SALES GOAL" example: "I would like to sell a lot and make a lot of money."
In either scenario, check off the requirements above and you will see that these examples fall short.

A GOOD "GOAL" SETTING example:
I am going on my dream vacation to Hawaii on January 1st of next year. I am saving $200 a month and will have the cost of the trip covered by that date. I also have a picture of this trip with the purchase date hanging on my mirror.

KEY 4 – FOCUS On Productivity

A GOOD "SALES GOAL" SETTING example: I am going to sell 4 accounts a quarter, each quarter this year. I will attain 110% of plan for the year. I will make $150,000 this year. I will be the # 1 rep in the company.

In these examples you can clearly see how these goals are real and have accountability measures. Studies have shown that people who actually set goals and have a goal planning process are more successful in attaining their goals than those who don't.

Goals should be a part of your daily plan. You should have goals set each day, week, month and year. Simply follow the components Check List on the previous page.

Don't Confuse Doing Activity with Sales Productivity.

This is another big one that can make or break your career.

Each day you will be confronted with many tasks and action items that will call for your attention. It is your job to be able to differentiate between Productivity and Activity.

Productivity pertains to those things (tasks, etc.) that are results impacting to your ability to generate sales.

Activity pertains to those things (tasks, etc.) that must be done, can be related to sales, but typically are not sales impacting at all.

A true sales professional is able to differentiate, categorize and prioritize the different action items that come up every day.

KEY 4 – FOCUS On Productivity

The key to effectively managing your day lies within adapting these principles as well:

#1. You must be able to identify and distinguish "Sales Impacting" items with "NON Sales Impacting" items and

#2. You must have a daily plan.

#3. You must take action.

In order to successfully complete this exercise, I encourage you to stop right now and get a pen and paper.

Why? Writing allows you to be involved with what you are doing and allows you to retain and better evaluate your information.

You will now need to make two columns.

Column 1 should be titled NON Sales Impacting: **Activity**

Column 2 should be titled Sales Impacting: **Productivity**

KEY 4 – FOCUS On Productivity

For the majority of sales professionals the Sales Impacting or Productivity Column is easy and will almost always include these standard items:

<u>Activity</u>	vs.	<u>Productivity</u>
Emails		Closing Sales Meetings
Making Follow-up calls		Attending Client Meetings
Building Client Files		Prospecting
Attending Networking Events		
Using Social Media		
Client Research on the Internet		
Completing Reports		

Let me clarify that the items listed in Column 1 are indeed important and they are a requirement for sales performance. However, for the sake of this exercise we are learning to categorize important tasks.

You should notice that in sales, the top 3 items of productivity are:

1. Closing Sales
2. Running Meetings
3. Prospecting

KEY 4 – FOCUS On Productivity

If you think in this manner and let your actions follow that same thought process, within a short time you will be able to be completely aware of non-productive tasks.

Earlier we talked about call reluctance. You will find that call reluctance is usually the main culprit behind doing unproductive sales tasks. This usually happens when you should be prospecting or setting meetings to grow your funnel.

If you don't know what to do, You will probably do something you shouldn't.

Measure Your Results.

This is a part of the science of sales. Since you are going to be an exceptional salesperson, it makes sense to know where you are, so you will know where you need to go. You will need to measure your progress along the way to see what is working and what isn't. We all have heard the definition of insanity: Doing the same thing over and over again, expecting different results. Well, don't be that person.

Keep track of your:
- Calls
- Call ratios
- Contacts to meetings and
- Presentations to closes

KEY 4 – FOCUS On Productivity

The day you take action to correct an ineffective behavior, your confidence will soar. You will be inspired to keep going and do more. You will be empowered to know that you have taken control of your sales career. You will manage your business instead of letting your business manage you. Performance plans and uncomfortable one-on-ones/reviews will be a thing of the past.

In fact, you will enjoy meeting with your manager to share your results.

KEY 4 SUMMARY

- ❖ **What is your plan to eliminate a "TRYING" mindset and move to one of commitment?**
- ❖ **Don't confuse activity with productivity.**
- ❖ **Write your daily plan with GOALS and present it to your manager for accountability.**
- ❖ **What is your plan to overcome Call Reluctance?**
- ❖ **Make note of unproductive daily activities that hold you back.**

KEY 5

PROSPECT Like You Are Competing

If you have ever really observed a normal sales team in action, you will find that most move through each day as if they were on a Sunday drive. They prospect at a leisurely rate of speed, and their results typically reflect their effort. You will also notice that the office tempo will only start to pick up or improve once the last week of the month has arrived.

This is a very stressful way to live, and some would call it self-destructive behavior.

I am comparing sales to driving, because we are in control of our destination. However, sales is really a performance based industry, like car racing. We are performance racers with a goal of winning. We are not leisurely drivers, hoping for something exciting to happen. We need to step up the tempo each day to ensure that we stay on pace to win every week, not just the last week. Think like a winner every day and let your prospecting be the fuel you need to perform like a champ.

KEY 5 – PROSPECT Like You Are Competing

The More You Sell, The More You'll Sell. The Less You Sell, The Less You'll Sell.

What that statement means is this: Sales is either a circle of productivity or a reverse circle of unproductivity. Everything starts with attitude.

1. **If you choose to have a great attitude, you will be more productive.**
2. **If you are more productive then you will set more meetings.**
3. **If you set more meetings you will close more opportunities.**
4. **If you close more opportunities you will make big commissions, and**
5. **If you make big commissions you will have a great attitude!**

Run this model in reverse and you will start to understand what I mean. In reverse, you will start to become less effective, because you will have less opportunities working. When you have less opportunities working, you become less effective, because you become more desperate and more emotionally attached to EACH SALE. You then are more inclined to do and say things that you normally wouldn't do and say, in a desperate attempt to get your sale. For example, a prospect might say to you: "This deal looks great, but can you lower your price?"

The wrong answer: "Absolutely, I can lower my price." This shows you have room to play and causes you to lose your leverage.

KEY 5 – PROSPECT Like You Are Competing

The right answer: "Based on your needs and your budget, the solution that I have prepared is actually right in line with where we both need to be." (Then you add a question).

Or the prospect might ask, "Can you get me a proposal this afternoon?"

The wrong answer: "Of course, I'll email it right over." Again, you look desperate and will lose your leverage.

The right answer: "I need to make sure that I can share the right solution for your needs. If I can get the pricing that we agreed to, are you in a position to meet with me this afternoon?"

When you respond confidently and show value for your time and for their time, people will respect your position. When you are living a reverse model of negativity, you look desperate, you will say things you normally wouldn't say and you might even act less confident. All of these things will cause you to lose your leverage, causing unnecessary delays and even lost sales. This will then compound the whole effect. You might have a tendency to become more emotionally attached to your opportunities, and as a result, you will be become very ineffective.

This is why it is very important to have multiple opportunities working all of the time. When you are relying on that "one deal" to get you to your quota, you will do and say things that you usually would not say.

Have a Prospecting Plan

Every morning that you wake up, I bet that you have the exact same routine. Think through your morning and you will agree.

KEY 5 – PROSPECT Like You Are Competing

Your routine will change periodically due to changes in your morning circumstances, but as a standard, your routine is the same.

Why is it the same? Because you are comfortable with it. Is it the most effective routine? It depends on the end result. If you are late to your destination frequently, I would say no. If you can comfortably walk through your routine and efficiently resolve each task, then you are probably good.

When it comes to prospecting, we need to adapt the same strategy. Have a prospecting plan and create a routine.

- ✓ Have a sense of urgency! Approach prospecting like a racing competition, not like Sunday drive!
- ✓ Know what you are going to do each day before your productive time starts and do it.
- ✓ Know if you will be in the field, on the phone, or on the internet prospecting or researching.

Cold Calling (Field Calls): Know where you are going. Know the businesses and addresses that you will call on. Also know what time you will get there and how long you will stay. If you have just made a sale, you might even go crazy and prospect around it.

Internet Research: This part can get tricky. We are a tech savvy society. We live on our electronics and mobile devices. Our brains have an association of engaging in personal activity, for most of us, when we are on them. If you have set a time for internet research, Google, general websites, etc., make sure that you have the discipline to be where you are and to actually do the research.

KEY 5 – PROSPECT Like You Are Competing

Research means looking up info about the companies and DMs that you will be calling on. Set a goal, a start time and an end time.

Focus on Getting People to Think "HMMM," Instead of Pushing Them for a Yes.

When my oldest daughter Lauren was about 6 years old, she asked to go with me on a trip to the grocery store. While we were walking down the cereal aisle she asked, "Daddy, can we buy another kind of cereal?" I responded quickly, "I don't think so sweetheart, not until the box at home is empty." She questioned, "But daddy, do you eat the same lunch and dinner every day?" I replied, "No," To which she questioned, "Well, why do you want me to eat the same breakfast every day?"

"Hmmm", I thought to myself.........she had sold me.

This is a sales strategy that I have used for years, after finding out that most salespeople are always "pushing" people to say yes.

Let me clarify that a "Yes" is always the end result of any sales process, but remember that you are managing a sales process and the more HMMMS, you get, the better chance that you will get a YES at the end of the process.

Getting HMMMs tells you that your prospect is interested. It tells you that something "makes sense" to them and that they want to learn more, without boxing the prospect into a corner. This in turn will allow you to share the value of your solution and eventually get them to say yes. Make sense? Of course.

KEY 5 – PROSPECT Like You Are Competing

Let's say you are talking with a prospect about a particular product on an initial call. Instead of going for the hard close and making the prospect feel uncomfortable, ask questions that generate a HMMM.

Wrong Approach – "Look at my product and see if you can fit it in your budget?"

Better Approach – "We have been able to help many businesses just like yours to improve their productivity. If we could show you a way to improve your productivity, you would at least look at it wouldn't you?"

The entire strategy of getting people to say HMMM, is the equivalent of getting your prospect to understand your concept or idea, and to think in their own mind that "this makes sense." If they understand, then they give you a verbal expression of YES to your concept or idea, NOT to buying your product.

Here is another example:

Mr. Prospect, invest 15 minutes with me so I can share with you how we have been helping businesses just like yours. If you see the value that we can provide for you, then we can go to the next step, if not, we can part friends, but at least you will know. Is that fair?

In this example, once again we are getting the prospect to say "HMMM" or agree to the idea that my "concept" is fair. They are not agreeing to buy from me, yet.

However, this first HMMM has now allowed me the golden opportunity to be a guest at their business, so I can share with them the value of my product or service in person.

KEY 5 SUMMARY

- ❖ Create a prospecting plan with targets that are challenging, but realistic to attain.
- ❖ Each day follow your prospecting plan.
- ❖ Are you spending too much time preparing?
- ❖ Focus on getting people to say **HMMM** instead of pushing for a Yes.

The more you sell,
The more you'll sell.
The less you sell,
The less you'll sell.

KEY 6

RUN Effective Client Meetings

Strategize Before Meetings.

If you are attending a meeting by yourself, get with your manager or a proven sales leader prior to going out to see your prospect. Give them an objective overview of where you are in the sales process, with no emotions, and get their feedback about your approach.

If you are going as a team, know who is going to lead and what your roles are. Decide what type of meeting it is and what your objectives are.

- Meeting Place - If you are going as a team, meet in the lobby or out front of the client's place of business. Do not go in until your entire team is there. Nothing is more distracting in a meeting than people walking in at random times after a meeting has started. The only exception is if someone is running more than 10 minutes late. Then go in and explain that he or she is on the way and will be joining soon. Another benefit of meeting together prior to a meeting, is that you can summarize your strategy.

KEY 6 – RUN Effective Client Meetings

- Assignments – If you have two or more people, identify the roles. Who will lead, etc.? If you have an engineer or a specialist, make sure that they only cover what they are there to cover. I have been at meetings where the rep walks in, introduces the sales engineer and looks at the engineer to run the meeting.

YOU are the salesperson. It's always your meeting. Run it!

- The "waiting" strategy – Everyone at some point has gone to see a prospect and had to sit and wait for a period of time. It is quite a pathetic sight when a prospect walks out after 30+ minutes to find a salesperson just sitting and waiting. You look desperate and will lose your leverage. I suggest that out of respect for your time (and to offset looking desperate), that you come up with a time limit for waiting. Mine is 12 minutes. If after 12 minutes a prospect does not show, I consider that they are too busy to meet with me. (Also understand that any time longer than this potentially runs over into your other meeting times.) I will approach the receptionist and say this: "I apologize, but it appears that Mr./Ms. ____ is busy right now. I am running a very tight meeting schedule today. My concern is that if we meet any later, that our meeting will run over into my next meeting, not allowing me to give Mr./Ms. Prospect the time and attention that they deserve. Out of respect for both of our time, can you please let them know that I will call back tomorrow to reschedule at a time that is more appropriate for them?"

KEY 6 – RUN Effective Client Meetings

The receptionist almost always apologizes, tells me that she understands and that she will tell Mr./Ms. Prospect that I will follow up.

With this strategy, when the prospect walks into the lobby, instead of seeing a desperate salesperson waiting for 30+ minutes, they are greeted by their receptionist who explains the situation. Now, when I call back, the prospect is very apologetic and will typically reschedule with me, usually more attentive because they feel bad. In this example, I am merely respecting my time and my prospects time.

Remember that you are a Prospect's Guest.

Several years ago I was investigating the option of purchasing a swimming pool for my house. I had reached out to several suppliers, conducted my initial interviews and set meetings with the finalists. On the day of one of the meetings, there was a knock at the door. I was on a phone call, however I carelessly opened the door and greeted the fellow. I motioned with my hand for him to wait. (I had just shampooed my carpets and I was going to ask him to remove his shoes.) He immediately and aggressively walked in, with dirty shoes, straight to my kitchen table.

I hung up the phone and apologized. I told him my intent was to ask him to remove his shoes. He responded that he didn't have time. I was shocked. He pulled out his demo book and attempted to go into a sales pitch. As quickly as he opened his book, I asked him to close it. Then I politely asked him to leave.

KEY 6 – RUN Effective Client Meetings

He seemed confused, but he did leave. This guy was clueless, because he was so focused on getting a sale. As a result, he was numb to the fact that he was in my home... as my guest. Since he didn't act like a guest, I asked him to leave AND without a sale I might add.

When you are visiting a client at their office, this same Key applies. You are still their guest. You must act in a way that is considerate and respectful of their time, their space and their requirements. This is accomplished by asking questions. You have the right to ask questions, because they did agree to meet with you. However, you never have the right to overstep your boundaries and say or do anything that would comprise being a guest in their space.

Remember they work there daily and they are aware of YOU and how you are conducting yourself.

Learn to Listen and Then Ask.

We have all heard that "Telling Isn't Selling" at some point in our career, yet most of us still do it. Why? Because we are salespeople and we like to talk.

What complicates this even more is that we have a tendency to incorrectly think that the more we talk, the more we are being received by the prospect. Even worse, we might even believe that we are sharing some profound and magnificent life changing information. This is usually not the case. In fact you will often get the opposite response.

I have determined that when you catch yourself talking too much, it's usually because you are uncomfortable.

KEY 6 – RUN Effective Client Meetings

The more we talk, the more comfortable we feel. To the contrary, the more words you use will usually have less of an impact.

When you are involved in conversation with a prospect, you must be aware of and be respectful of their time. By talking with a great amount of words and talking too much, you will lose your effect.

Let me use an example of less is more. Mike Tyson was a great fighter. He won many fights because his focus was to deliver select, strategic and powerful blows. Each one with a precise cause and goal: to knock out his opponent. He didn't get in the ring and start swinging multiple small punches all over the place. This would have exhausted him, causing his opponent frustration. It might have even leveraged them to win.

One way that you can measure the success of a meeting, is to evaluate who is talking the most. If it is you, then you will have problems. We do not TELL people solutions. We determine solutions by uncovering pain points, problems or needs, by strategically asking questions, effectively listening to the prospects answers and confirming what we have heard. We then ask more questions relative to those options, listen again and repeat the cycle until the client is comfortable that we understand their needs or pains.

It is only when you really understand the prospects pain or needs that you can start "talking" to share the value, features or benefits of your proposed solution. If you ask strategic and meaningful questions to help you uncover your prospects needs, you will win more opportunities.

When you feel the urge to purge your words, just turn your phrase into a question!

KEY 6 – RUN Effective Client Meetings

He Who Asks Questions, Manages the Conversation.

I'm not saying that you need to be in full control of a meeting, what I am saying is that you need to manage your own sales process out of respect for your prospect and for your own sanity. It seems simple enough, but it is harder than you think, especially if you have been a "talking" salesperson for any period of time.

Asking questions is a critical part of the Art of Sales. It isn't about starting an interrogation or being intrusive. It's about managing the conversation. You manage the conversation to allow your prospect to do most of the talking, so that YOU can listen and learn more from their words.

The reason you want the prospect to talk more is so that you can get them to communicate what they are thinking. You need to know what's going on in their mind, so you can understand, see if you are a fit and overcome objections.

Let's look at a few examples.

Wrong Way: "Glad you are meeting with me, we have a fantastic product and I just love it."

Better: "Thank you for investing your time in meeting with me. What is the main solution that you are looking to provide for your company?"

When you ask questions and then cease talking, you show that you are listening. You convey that the prospect's needs are important to you. This will also give you a chance to really listen. Then, based on the prospect's response, you can craft another question to understand them even more.

KEY 6 – RUN Effective Client Meetings

You will often meet with prospects who like to talk. Let them talk. You can learn quite a bit from hearing what your prospect says. The more questions you ask that are in direct response to what your prospect has just said, the more progress you will make.

Ask Open Ended Questions, Like WHY?

"WHY" is probably the most under used word by adults. In contrast it is probably one of the most frequently used words by children. Why? Because children are curious. They are not too proud to learn. They want to learn and they will break down each layer of each answer that you provide. They will keep asking again and again until you provide a reasonable explanation that satisfies their curiosity.

Adults on the other hand, usually don't want to come across as being ignorant or deficient on a subject or situation. Some will go along with the conversation, only to leave and then Google the answers. Borrow this strategy from children and use this very powerful word "WHY." It is a very simple, but a very powerful word.

There are other words that are part of the open ended question family: Who, what, when and where. You must know that there is a proper way to use open ended questions. Here it is: You ask it and then you zip your lips and listen. You will be amazed at how much you learn.

Example:

A prospect gives you an objection and tells you that they are unsure about your offer.

KEY 6 – RUN Effective Client Meetings

Wrong Answer – "Well it is a great service and we have many happy clients AND we offer a guarantee."

Better Answer – "My apologies, apparently I missed something. Can you please help me? You said that you are unsure about my offer? **What** specifically about my offer is it that you are unsure about?"

Asking open ended questions and then closing your mouth and listening, is really the true and simple way to learn and handle objections.

A closed ended question will only generate a Yes or a NO, which in turn will halt the conversation in its footsteps.

Another example:

Closed Ended:

YOU: "Do you like Ice Cream?" (Zip it) Prospect: "Yes."

YOU: "Great, What kind do you like?"

This example is a two-step process that is long and cumbersome to your prospect

Open Ended:

YOU: What kind of Ice cream do you like?

Again practice this art until you can internalize the flow, so that the two-step questioning process is avoided.

KEY 6 – RUN Effective Client Meetings

Answer a Question With a Question.

Nothing in this book is intended to manipulate anyone! Our sole purpose is always to help our prospects. In order to effectively assist, it is important that we understand and overcome objections. To understand you must ask questions. Therefore, if someone asks you a question, you should acknowledge their question and then ask a question back to clarify their request. This is an ART!!! You must practice your delivery. This is not an interrogation. As I mentioned earlier, this must be internalized and delivered sincerely.

Example 1: Client question: "Can you tell me more about the features?"

Wrong Answer: "YES! Of course..." (And then start incessantly rambling about the product information)

Right Answer: "Of course, to help me better understand your needs, what specific features would you like to learn more about?"

Example 2: Client Question: "What makes you better than the competition?"

Wrong Answer: Start again with incessant rambling of how great you are or how bad the competition is.

Right Answer: "That is a great question. What are the most important things that you expect from your next provider/company?"

This approach would then allow you to cover on the details that are important to your client, not the details that YOU feel are important.

KEY 6 – RUN Effective Client Meetings

A strategic tip: if you are asked a question and you don't know what to say, you say this:

"That's a great, question… Let me ask you a question"

Here is the art. When you say to someone, "Let me ask you a question," their senses adapt as they prepare to listen to your question. There is actually a very brief, split second of blankness in their mind, as they prepare to listen.

Here is the strategy. When they stop and look at you and listen for that brief, split second, it gives you the opportunity to actually think of a great question that is relative to understanding THEIR question better. This can help you to progress the sale. The goal is to continue to ask in a conversational way until you understand fully what the prospect needs. You must always conduct yourself with integrity and honesty. If they ask you a question and you don't know the answer, just respond with this: "That is a great question. Let me write that down to make sure I can get you the right answer."

KEY 6 – RUN Effective Client Meetings

When You Ask a Question, Don't Give Answers.

This is a major problem with people in general, but especially with salespeople.

I have experienced through observation at many sales appointments, that some salespeople just cannot adopt this strategy.

An example:

A prospect might make the statement, "We are currently having service problems." The salesperson should ask, "When you say service problems, can you please explain or tell me what you mean?" And then zip their lips. BUT, most salespeople will keep going and offer answers like these: "Are they not calling you? Is the service bad?" They continue to ask without even allowing the client to explain. Sometimes the salesperson will even fire off multiple answers as options, one right after the other.

Another example:

We ask a question: "So what kind of services are you looking to buy?" (And then we proceed to give our answers, instead of waiting and listening to hear the prospects answers)... "Are you looking for this, or that, or the other?" All while the prospect just stares at us.

When you ask a question, ask it and then completely close your mouth. Then discipline yourself to resist the temptation to volunteer any options.

With this approach, you cause the prospect to actually think about what they are going to say, so you can actually hear their true concerns or needs. It is harder than it seems, but with practice, you can do it.

KEY 6 – RUN Effective Client Meetings

You must also practice this in your daily life to perfect it. An ideal way to practice is to ask questions to your family or friends and then close your mouth and listen. Resist the temptation to give options for THEIR answers!

As a salesperson, I know that we love to hear ourselves talk, but you must remember that sales is not about us. It is always about the prospect. Think of it this way: when you volunteer your own answers after you have asked a question to someone else, you are actually preventing them from thinking on their own. Since they are not giving you their own thoughts, how in the world can you understand what they are thinking? You have also made it very difficult to provide the right solution.

When you volunteer answers to your own questions, you create a big risk. Some people might actually agree with one of your answers, causing you to believe you have the right information. This type of practice is not effective and will not produce the best results. You cannot create a need.

Only ask one question at a time. Give people the opportunity to answer your questions and give yourself the opportunity to actually listen to what they are saying!

A final note:

When you are at the point when you are responding to your prospect's questions about your product or service, you need to clarify that you have answered their question. Here is how: After you answer their question, you ask them: "Does that make sense?" Or "Did I provide you with the answer that you were looking for?" It is important to follow up and show that you are indeed interested in and concerned about providing the right information to address their concerns or objections.

KEY 6 – RUN Effective Client Meetings

Pay Less Attention to the Words That People Use and MORE Attention to Why They are Saying Them.

For those of you who are married or dating, I'm sure there has been a time that you and your partner have escalated a conversation from debate to argument.

Most arguments are usually never resolved because both parties are intent on proving their point and usually neither will acknowledge the point of view of the other. By the way, so now that you know how arguments are escalated, start listening to your partner's point of view and acknowledge it. This will minimize arguments in your relationship!

There is another very important element that is often overlooked:

Words.

Words are merely an expression of our thoughts.

If you can think of a time when you miscommunicated your thoughts by using the wrong words, then you will understand what I am saying. Words can be misleading. It is important to focus on the thought behind the words, so you can tune into the person you are talking with. This will get you both on the same page.

For example, if you come home tomorrow and your spouse starts griping and complaining:

KEY 6 – RUN Effective Client Meetings

"Why didn't you pick up your laundry today!? You always leave your clothes lying around the house!"

The typical person perceives this as an attack, reacts and replies back with something unproductive like, "Well if you would clean the laundry, I would have a place to keep my clothes."

This type of reaction to the other person's "words" causes escalation and poor results.

Now, what if you were to listen to WHY your spouse was saying these words:

"Why didn't you pick up your laundry today!? You always leave your clothes lying around the house!"

If you focus on WHY, you can clearly hear that your spouse is really saying, "I had a stressful day and I need your help!"

In this instance, you can now RESPOND, instead of reacting, by saying "Sweetheart, I'm very sorry, I can see how that is frustrating. Let me pick up my clothes. Is there anything else I can do to help?"

You can now see that your attitude and HIS/HER attitude would create different results for both of you. This would contribute to a healthier relationship.

So how does this translate to sales? Easy. When a prospect says, "We need more time to evaluate your offer," you now know that what they are really saying is, "We don't see the full value and we need to evaluate and/or learn more before we make a decision."

This approach will then allow you to respond accordingly. You can then pursue the best possible outcome to address their needs. It takes hours of listening practice to get this down, but if you are determined, you can do it.

KEY 6 – RUN Effective Client Meetings

Presenting Proposals.

There is an art to presenting a proposal. The more complicated that you make your proposal; the more complex your prospect will make the actual review of your proposal. This will affect the outcome of your sales process. You must understand what a proposal is and what it isn't.

What it is: A summary of your proposed solution, with the associated price/investment for your proposed solution.

What it isn't: a sales presentation book. It shouldn't be a continuation of your sales process or a complete overview of everything that you have reviewed up to this point. Brochures and proposals are sales tools. Not Salespeople.
Your proposal should never be a complex document or a book of sales brochures, unless you want a complex sales process. You should never rely on a proposal to sell for you.

NOTES:
- A proposal should never be presented until you have effectively qualified the opportunity.
- It should only be presented when you are at the final stages of sharing the proposed solution and the investment associated with that solution.

Brochures are sales tools,
Not Salespeople.
Your proposal should never be a
complex document,
Unless you want a
complex sales process.
You shouldn't rely on either
to sell for you.

KEY 6 – RUN Effective Client Meetings

YOU are the salesperson and your proposal is a summary of your solution.
DO NOT rely on your proposal to do the selling for you.
This is a major mistake.

NEVER mail or email a proposal, unless you are dealing with someone you cannot meet with or someone who is unable to meet with you face to face.
A proposal is a summary of all of the work that you have done. You must be the one presenting it, so if they have any more questions, you will be there physically, with your prospect, to answer those questions. When you send or give a prospect a proposal without presenting it to them, you are in fact removing yourself from the sales process. Once you have removed yourself from the sales process the odds of you actually getting the sale have decreased from slim to none.
When you leave a proposal with a prospect without answering questions, the prospect will then come to their own conclusion based on the information that you have provided. It may or may not be the right conclusion.

When you change your views about what a proposal is and what it isn't, you can be better prepared to present your proposal to get the best results.

We Propose to Close!

KEY 6 – RUN Effective Client Meetings

"THANK YOU" the Positive Ending to a Meeting.

When I get up to leave a meeting, I always continue to listen and watch. If my prospect has become my client, then I know 100% that they will thank me. However, if we have a "Maybe," a method I use to see if we will progress the meeting, is to simply check if they "Thank me."

If they thank me, I know that they see value in the time they have invested with me. A Thank You means that they have seen the value of your thoughts, words, actions and considerations, relative to the solution they see for their needs or pains.

I encourage you to manage your words, actions, thoughts and behaviors to generate a "thank you" each time you get the privilege to interact with a prospect.

KEY 6 SUMMARY

- ❖ Why is it important to plan and strategize before your meetings?
- ❖ Learn to listen and then ask questions.
- ❖ Ask open ended questions, then be quiet!
- ❖ Practice asking questions without giving answers.
- ❖ Practice presenting your proposals as a closing tool.

KEY 7

MANAGE Your Sales Process

Yes every sale has a process and yes someone needs to manage it. That someone is ALWAYS you.

In order to understand the sales process, you must understand sales components. Let's cover them now, starting with...

Know the Definition of a Meeting.

Meeting: A specific time and date, with a qualified prospect, to meet with a Decision Maker (DM) or an impact DM at a place where they typically conduct business.

If you are in sales, every sales opportunity and every sales process, starts with a meeting with your prospect. For the sake of this book, we are primarily referencing face to face meetings, but for those of you in telesales, you can also make note of a meeting definition.

The reason a meeting definition is important, is because if you know what a meeting is, then it is easier to know what a meeting isn't.

KEY 7 – MANAGE Your Sales Process

There are many false sales opportunities out there that exist in the minds of some salespeople. If you dig deeper on some of these opportunities, you will find that an actual meeting has never even taken place.

All elements of the "Meeting Definition" must be present in order for YOU to classify your prospect meeting as a true meeting. Otherwise, you probably only had an encounter or just a casual conversation.

When you attend a meeting in person, there are more strategies that you must follow:

There Are Only 3 Kinds of Meetings.

1. **1st Meeting –** This is always a discovery meeting. It can be very long or very short depending on the sales situation and/or the product/solution that you are selling. A discovery meeting is simply to discover the details of why your prospect is meeting with you.
   We usually don't close or propose on a discovery meeting (however you might, depending on your industry).
   If handled properly, a discovery meeting will transition into a Follow-up Meeting or a series of Follow-up Meetings, each with a specific action. The main plan to follow for a discovery meeting is this: ASK QUESTIONS! This is a time for you to learn about your prospect, their business, their goals and their challenges. It is also a time for your prospect to learn about you. Ask, listen and take notes!

KEY 7 – MANAGE Your Sales Process

The best openers for first meetings!

    a. If you visit clients in the field, ask: "Besides my phone call, what prompted you to meet with me today?" – Then you zip it and listen. 9 out of 10 times they will start to tell you the honest reason.

    b. If you meet with clients at a store, ask: "Besides looking, what prompted you to come in today?" – Then you zip it and listen. 9 out of 10 times they will start to tell you the honest reason.

2. **Follow Up Meeting** – If you haven't heard of my system before, this way of thinking might be different. You can have many Follow-up meetings, however, each one will have a specific action that will take place during each meeting.

   By following this process you can effectively categorize your meetings and then review your plan of action at each meeting as you progress.

   Example: I have attended a discovery meeting.
   During the discovery meeting, two things happened:
       a) I learned that the prospect was looking to add new products or services.
       b) We scheduled a **1st Follow-up** meeting Thursday at 10 am to review available options.

   At the end of the **1st Follow-up**, our next step would be to schedule a **2nd Follow-up** meeting to present those options.

   Using this system, each time you "**Follow-up**" you will have a specific "action" at each meeting.

KEY 7 – MANAGE Your Sales Process

This system will also let you understand, manage and progress your sales cycle. It is basically a system of next steps. Each step with specific action items for you AND your prospect.

3. **Closing Meeting** – After you have had a discovery and 1, 2 or multiple follow up meetings, depending on your prospects needs or requirements, you will be at the point where you should have covered the 6 required component of the sales process (covered next).

   When managing your current opportunities, if you "THINK," "FEEL," or "WOULD LIKE," for them to close, they usually won't.
   Remember it is never about you!

There Are Only 3 Outcomes of Meetings.

You will either get a Yes, a No or you will schedule a next meeting to progress the sale. I have found that this is a very difficult concept for salespeople to grasp, because we have a hard time getting or accepting the word NO. NO's are good. When people tell you "maybe" you must understand that they are saying "NO" or YES with conditions! In other words, they don't see the value of your offer. So consider the following as the 3 only possible outcomes of a sales meeting. You must understand these and live by this process. Internalize this so you will know where you stand:

1. **You get a YES /CLOSE.** This means that they like it and they see the value. You both have agreed to conduct business together and sign paperwork at an agreed upon date and time.

2. **You get a NO/DON'T CLOSE.** They don't see the value or it may not be a fit. Either way you both have agreed that you WILL NOT conduct business together at this time.
NOTE: "Maybe" is not an outcome. You will need to work on this, as we tend to take "maybe' as a yes. Change your thinking to "Maybe" is a yes or a no, with conditions." A "Maybe" means more work needs to be done.

3. **You schedule a Follow-up Meeting** – to address the conditions of the "maybe" and or to continue to establish value and to address their concerns or solve their pain/need.
Note: If a prospect doesn't see value in your offer, they will not set a follow-up meeting with you.

The 6 Required Components of Every Sale:

I don't like to deal with acronyms, so you will need to internalize (not remember) these 6 required components.

I have travelled across the US extensively, met with companies of all sizes from 1 owner shops to fortune 100. Through my experience and research I have concluded that every potential sales opportunity must have these 6 components outlined and resolved, in order for value to be created and the sale to be closed. There are always other variables or details that are sales impacting, but I can assure you that any one of those variables will inevitably fall within 1 of these 6 components:

KEY 7 – MANAGE Your Sales Process

1. **Must have a Pain or Need –**

    If a prospect does not have a pain or a need, they will usually not buy from you.

    PAIN: DO NOT confuse "PAIN" with a potential "PROBLEM." The "pain" is the actual RESULT of their problem. If someone has slow internet service, it might be frustrating (a Problem), but it might not necessarily be painful for them. The Pain would be the actual RESULT of the slow internet. So a great question to ask would be: How is that pain (slow internet) affecting/impacting your business? They might tell you that they are unable to access information and as a result they are losing clients. This would create a financial impact. Don't confuse a problem with an actual pain. Remember pain is business impacting!

    NEED:

    If your prospect doesn't have a pain, but they have a need, they are still in the game. A need is the desire or requirement to have something that can impact their business. For example, a "need" might be to have a software based accounting system if they are using manual books. It is always your job to uncover the potential NEEDS or the actual PAINS for each of your prospects.

Remember, if a prospect does not have a pain or a need, they usually won't buy from you.

2. **Decision Making – Who is the Decision Maker/Who is the Signer/What is the DM Process/What is the DM Time frame**

   The Decision Maker is the person who will ultimately choose the solution. They have the final say. They may or may not be the signer.

   The Signer is the person who will actually sign the paperwork. You know this because they have TOLD YOU. Now sometimes people aren't completely honest, but that is an exception not the standard. Remember, in this book, we follow the standards. This may or may not be the Decision Maker!

   The DM Process is the process by which they make the decision to get your value proposition or proposed solution to the person who will sign the paperwork.

   The DM time frame is the period of time, with a target date, that they plan to get to the signer to actually sign the paperwork. All four are different, but they work together. All four must be present and accounted for in order to close a deal. Many times you will work with an impact decision maker. This is fine, as long as you understand the decision making process and clarify who it is that will actually sign.

KEY 7 – MANAGE Your Sales Process

3. **What is their Budget (Not Price)**
   Can they afford it and do they have the ability to buy it.
   Everyone has a budget when it comes to making a purchase. If you don't believe me just think about your last car purchase and why you didn't buy a Ferrari (I just made you say HMMM).

   Budget is the financial amount the prospect is willing or is able to pay for a product or service.
   Most people will have a "high" over their budget – that they are willing to pay, and a "low" that they would like to or would prefer to pay.
   Their budget will likely fall in the middle. You must know their budget.

   Budget is very different from price.

   Price is the amount that YOU are offering for your product or service. Example: Let's say that a prospect is looking to buy a new car and has a budget of $25K. You bring out a top of the line pre-owned Mercedes with a sticker price of $75K. You offer incentives to get the price down to $65K. This really excites you, as the salesperson, because this is now a really fantastic price for this car.
   Unfortunately the prospect still won't buy. Why?
   The budget!!

KEY 7 – MANAGE Your Sales Process

Although the PRICE was amazing, it still is not in line with the prospects budget: what they are willing or able to pay.

When you are working with your prospect, the price that you give, even if it is a tremendous savings, might not necessarily win the deal if it is not in line with their budget.

Budget is different than price and it must be uncovered, so that you can find the right solution that is in line with what they have allocated to pay.

4. **What Solution do they need? Can you provide it?** Are you offering a solution that YOU think they want or need? Maybe you just want them to buy so you can make quota.

    Offer them the right solution for the pain or need that they have. Is the prospect looking for a camping stove? Then don't sell them a microwave. You must propose a solution that addresses their pain and provides a solution specific to their need. This is another reason why sales are lost. We attempt to squeeze a prospect into a cool solution that is not the solution that they need.

    When you have managed your sales process and uncovered their pain and their budget, you should be proposing the right solution, if you can provide it.

    If so, you will then propose and recap the benefits of how this solution can improve their situation and remove their pain.

5. **When do they need it?** If they haven't specified or agreed to a current time or date that they need your service or product, there will not be an incentive to buy now. In this case, you might need to create a sense of urgency, if they see the value. However, you might uncover and effectively address all 4 steps above, but if they do not need the solution until a later date, due to contractual obligations or other, then they will not buy today or within YOUR time frame.

6. **Next Steps: Specific Date and Time, Plan of Action.** This is the true litmus test. If you have effectively addressed or are addressing all of the above 5 steps, the client will set a next step/next meeting with you to continue towards their buying decision. If they do not or will not set a follow up meeting, you are missing something in the 5 steps! Apparently they do not see the value and therefore they will not be willing to go to the next step with you. It is at this point that you will need to identify where you are in the sales process, where your client is and make sure that both of you get on the same page.

When all of these sales steps are worked together successfully, they create value for your prospect. If your prospect sees value, they will buy. If they don't see value, they won't buy.

KEY 7 – MANAGE Your Sales Process

A Story about Value

Here is an example in that is easy to understand and it just makes sense. Here you go:

Let's say a door to door salesperson comes to your front door tonight and knocks. You open the door and see a professionally dressed salesperson who proceeds to share their intro sales pitch with you. You seem to like them as they ask you questions that get you to say, HMMM. You develop a sense of trust, so you invite them into the front room of your house. You sit down and they ask you more questions to learn about your needs. They start to share with you the benefits of their service and how it can provide a solution to your needs. You look at your spouse, who is with you, and you both agree without a doubt, that this is 100% a service that can provide a benefit to your life. You then ask the salesperson, "How much is it?" The salesperson confidently responds, "That is the best part, how much would you expect it to cost?" You say I don't know, maybe about "X" amount of dollars. The salesperson then quotes you the price. You look at your wife and you both agree that the price is in line or below what you expected to pay, considering the value. In fact you have the funds in your budget to pay right now and the purchase will not impact your financial situation.

Here is the question: When do you buy?

Honest answer: Right then. WHY? Because...

People buy when they see value.

So do you. That is why this story makes perfect sense. It also proves to you that if people like and trust you, as long as you show value, if you can meet their budget and if all decision makers are available, that they will buy.

Use a Risk/Benefit Assessment for Tough Decisions.

This is a great tool for decision making that you can use for almost every aspect of your life.

I must caution you that when you use this type of assessment that you must be "completely" honest. You must also remove your emotions and ONLY deal with the real facts and potential outcomes of the situation. This is how it works: Consider your decision that you are thinking about making. Now do a deep dive to determine what the risks are? When I say risks, this is what I mean. How will making the decision affect your life or someone else's life? Can it possibly affect you or others adversely or negatively? Also, you must consider the residual impact as well.

If you are considering taking a new job that pays a higher salary than what you currently make, the higher salary might be very appealing.

However, after conducting a risk assessment, you might determine that the risk is that you will have to travel 80% of the time which might be too much travel for you. In addition, you might determine that the residual risk is that you will be away from your family and that your absence will put unnecessary stress on your family, life and/or marriage.

The conclusion in this case would be that the Risks clearly outweigh the Benefit of more money.

The new job might not be worth it.

A risk assessment is also a great tool when evaluating sales opportunities. It can help you to determine when to take action when you are planning your daily productivity tasks.

KEY 7 – MANAGE Your Sales Process

In "sales" a risk/benefit assessment is perfect when making sales impacting decisions:

- **When to email vs. making a live call,**
- **Phone meetings vs. live meetings**
- **Haven't heard back, when should I call?**
- **Should I include incentives or not?**
- **Waiting on a deal vs. prospecting**

THINK: LET'S DO *THIS*.....

Where are you in your sales process? When you engage with a potential prospect, your goal is to work through the sales process with them.

Forward Thinking means thinking about solutions that will get you to the next steps with your prospect. It means moving forward with your prospects needs and pains in mind. It means keeping them in the sales process with you, so you can take them to the point where you can provide a solution to their needs.

If you are stuck and you need to establish the next steps or plan of action, simply say:

"Mr./Mrs. Prospect, Let's do *this*"

Saying "Let's do *this*" addresses the fact that you are both in "*this*" together. It shows that you aren't just thinking about you.

KEY 7 – MANAGE Your Sales Process

If a prospect says that they are interested, but they need 2 references, there are two ways to handle this:

1. Not the best way - "Ok let me check and see and I'll get back with you soon." This is not forward thinking. You have put the sales process on hold and are no longer linear thinking.

2. A Better Way – "Let's do *this*…. I will get you the 2 references. Is that all you need to finalize your decision?"

This is forward thinking. If they say yes, then you agree to a date and time for the next steps.

If you are a forward thinking salesperson, you are always establishing the next steps, clarifying action items and making things happen.

You are preventing them from making unnecessary delays.

Linear Thinking with your prospect means to imagine your sales process as a line, with a point "A" (First Meeting) and a point "Z" (Closing Meeting). Your goal is to follow a progression of steps, to move forward from your first meeting until you get a yes or a no, "WITH your prospect." You do this to ensure that your prospect is at the exact same place that you are in the sales process at the same time. Linear thinking prevents people from getting side-tracked.

KEY 7 – MANAGE Your Sales Process

Example of managing a sales process together shown by symbols, which indicate where each person is in the process:

YOU= ◌   **Your Prospect =** ◊

<u>Discovery, Follow-up Q&A, Follow-up to Propose/Close</u>

Example of an unbalanced sales process:

Discovery---→--◊Follow-up-----→---◌Propose/Close-----Z

Example of a balanced sale process:

Discovery---→---Follow-up---→----◊◌Propose/Close-----Z

The benefit of thinking linear, is that you can visualize where you are in the sales process. At the same time, you can also know where your prospect is. If your prospect tells you that they have more questions for you, and YOU are expecting to close, you know that you need to slow down and back up to where they are in the sales process.

The strategy and art of thinking together, ensures that you both are at the same place at the same time. Therefore you can work together to find and get the right solution.

You Must Level-Set Situations That Need It.

No one has more value than you and no one is better than you. Likewise you are not better than anyone else.

I have worked with small business owners and I have worked with multi-millionaires. They both have one thing in common. They wake up in the morning just like you.

KEY 7 – MANAGE Your Sales Process

I have mentioned many times that according to Ziglar, "Sales isn't something that you do to someone, it's something that you do for and with someone." This also applies to your prospects dealing with you. You should treat people with respect and YOU should be treated respectfully.

I have often found that for some reason, some salespeople feel that they are not as good as other people when in a business situation. They think that they are not worthy.

Our profession is a noble profession. I'm confident that there are more millionaires produced out of the sales profession than out of any other profession. Once you can understand this, you must start thinking of yourself as a true sales professional, because you are. After all, you are paid to sell.

You will meet people who will want to talk down to you and tell you what to do and dictate how business will be conducted. This is usually on their terms.

Know this:

We sell to people and not buildings. Faces and not places.

Never be intimidated and never act or come across with anything less than 100% confidence (not arrogance), kindness and professionalism.

You will find that "level-setting" a situation, only requires this: Make sure that your words, eye contact, actions and responses are on the exact same level as the person you are talking with.

KEY 7 – MANAGE Your Sales Process

You must be respected, and you must also always show respect. Do not let a title, a position or a wealthy disposition make you unbalanced. Make sure that you level-set when you need to.

The Y Factor:
Thinking Yes or No, to Improve Your Results.

I have learned that almost every situation in life has a yes or a no, a positive or a negative. You are living or you are dead, you work or you don't, people buy or they don't. It's that simple and you must believe it. Even if you do something part time or some of the time, you are either doing it or not doing it. If you show up to a job, but aren't working then you aren't working, regardless of the fact that you are there physically.

It's not the amount of time that is the issue, it's the action and mindset of what it is that you are doing in general.

The word "maybe" should never be accepted as finality.

KEY 7 – MANAGE Your Sales Process

With the "Y" Factor, the bottom stem of the "Y" represents decisions in every situation in your life. The stem extending to the left hand side represents a "NO" and the stem extending to the right hand side will represent "YES." The middle of the V represents "Maybe."

NO   MAYBE   YES

DECISION

You must learn to identify these as your primary alternatives and by default you will become more effective in listening and in making decisions.

KEY 7 – MANAGE Your Sales Process

Maybe is either a NO or a conditional YES. Ill repeat that:

Maybe is a NO, OR it can be a YES…with conditions.

Here is an Example: You ask a friend to take a trip with you to Hawaii. They will typically say Yes, No or Maybe. If they say yes, of course they are going. If they tell you No, well then they aren't going. In both of these cases, you know where they stand and so do they. However, if they say "maybe," which is in the grey area, this is where we start to get lost and lose direction. This is why it is so important to understand thy Y Factor, so you will know where you stand. You must question them (skillfully) and ask why?

Here are some examples of responses to clarify "Maybe."

- Maybe with a conditional yes: They might say "I want to go, but I'm broke. If you can pay for the trip for me, then I will go." The answer here was a yes. They want to go with the condition that you will finance the trip. If that condition isn't met, then they cannot go.

- Maybe as a No: They might say, "Thank you for asking, let me think about it, but I'll get back with you on that." In this case the answer is probably no, but they don't want to tell you no. It could be for any variety of reasons. However, the answer is still no, but is being presented to you as a Maybe.

As a sales professional, it is your job to understand the difference and to learn what those conditions are. You must be able to provide a solution that the client can agree to and that they can understand.

If you cannot provide an effective solution or resolve a pain or need, then you will get a "maybe" or even a full blown NO.

KEY 7 – MANAGE Your Sales Process

Look at the process from this perspective. If you call a prospect, they will either:

A) Meet with you, or B) Not meet with you.

If they do meet with you, they will either:

A) See the value of your offer, or B) Not see the value.

If they see they value, they will either:

A) Afford it or B) Not afford it….and so on.

Learn to think this way and you will know how to respond to situations when you are listening to your prospects.

The end result: When you are dealing with a prospect or a person that tells you "maybe," it is not a bad thing. It simply means that you have more work to do to understand their concerns or conditions, so you can share with them the value of your offer. If they tell you no, at least you will know where you stand and then you can move on to the next prospect.

In addition, when someone gives you a NO, that isn't necessarily a bad thing either. People do not like to hear the word "no" and salespeople cringe when we do.

Here are a few reasons why getting a "NO" is a good thing:

- **You know where you stand**
- **You can move on**
- **You can take it out of your funnel**
- **You might be able to overcome the true objection**

When a prospect tells you No and you accept it, an amazing thing happens. The sales process is over. You can now treat them as an individual instead of a prospect, and they will view you as a person instead of someone trying to sell them something. Now that their guard is down, just say this: "Thank you for giving me the chance to earn your business, and I appreciate your decision. Can I ask you one question before I leave?"

"What is it that we didn't do or could have done to put you in a position to earn your business?" Usually, since they no longer view you as a salesperson, they will tell you the reason why.

Guess what happens next? You will know the reason why they didn't buy, and now you can start your sales process back up with them.

Use "Time" Wisely When Dealing with Prospects.

This is not about time management, although time management is critical. I'm talking about using your time effectively, as a tool when working with your prospects.
Let's say that you have presented to a prospect and you haven't established a specific next step. You are now waiting to hear back from them (this is ineffective process management).

Every day that goes by, you are losing time, your valuable time. While you are losing time, you are also losing your value to the prospect and your leverage with the prospect. In these types of situations, time will kill your sales.

Likewise, if a prospect is asking you to send information and you send that information immediately, without prequalifying the reason for the sense of urgency, you have just misused your time. As a result, your time will betray you. Your desperation to get a sale has now been exposed.

Use your time wisely. Calculate when and how you will respond to requests.

BIG FOOT Hunting / Emotional Selling
Don't Become Emotionally Attached to Sales.

Let's face it, when you don't have any sales, you lose your confidence.

Lack of confidence leads to poor judgment, poor decisions, and poor results. If you are working with a prospect and you aren't sure if you are managing your sales process, or if you are emotionally attached to the sale, simply ask these questions:

- Do I have a specific next meeting (Time and Date) set up with a specific next step or a specific plan of action?
- Am I waiting on them to call me?
- Have they asked me to call them sometime in the future without a specific date agreed by both parties?
- Have I used any of these emotional words:
    - I **hope** it will come in
    - I **think** it will come in
    - I **feel** good about it
    - Kinda...
    - They really **like** me
    - I'm **pretty sure** that they will do it
    - They are **supposed** to do it
    - My **gut tells me** so, or
    - That's **just the way** they do business.

KEY 7 – MANAGE Your Sales Process

If you have used any of these words then you are running your business emotionally.

An emotionally attached salesperson defends the prospect and the prospect's unreasonable requests or lack of response. They linger around the office talking about these opportunities they have working, as if they are valid. However, they cannot discuss any specific next steps and usually don't have a follow up meeting scheduled or any specific details to progress the opportunity. Then, after the client finally reveals the NO, they now mope around the office, complaining about the deal they lost. HEADS UP! You can't lose something you never had.

I call these BIG FOOT DEALS. Big Foot deals are opportunities that are often talked about, sometimes for months, but no one ever sees them. They are never brought in.

If you are not emotionally attached, you will respect your prospects time AND your own time! You will also be able to think and act clearly in a way that progresses your sales process and keeps you and your prospect on the same page, even if this means getting a "NO" as an answer.

Stop "Waiting" for opportunities to come in!

KEY 7 SUMMARY

- ❖ What is the definition of a "true" meeting?
- ❖ Map out and understand the sales process.
- ❖ Why is a sales process beneficial?
- ❖ What are the 6 required components of every sale?
- ❖ Are you creating value or are you pushing what you need the prospect to buy?
- ❖ Are you a **BIG FOOT HUNTER?**

KEY 8

BELIEVE You Are Exceptional

Through Faith and Action, All Things are Possible.

You must have faith and you must take action when a situation calls for you to change to become better.

Faith is the belief that your plan or goals will happen. Faith is the fuel that prompts you to action.

Action creates the steps that are needed to get you where you plan or need to go.

As you continue your journey and encounter failures, your faith will empower you to get back up, keep going and focus on your goals in a new and different light.

When you regain your power and your confidence, you will take action again and again.

By doing this, you will increase your chances to succeed.

If you have ever seen or experienced a sand storm, you know that it is a very frightening situation. As the cloud of sand engulfs the individual, their main senses are almost completely cut off. The person becomes disoriented and fear immediately

KEY 8 – BELIEVE You Are Exceptional

takes over and escalates the situation very quickly. They cannot see, cannot hear and can barely breathe, completely unaware of which direction to go. It is completely overwhelming.

However, it is only through faith and action that you can survive a sandstorm. Your faith tells you that the sandstorm will end and that you can survive if you choose to. Action prompts you to do the critical things necessary to ensure your ability to survive.

You must have faith and you must take action to pursue your goals. You must believe that you can accomplish your goals through faith and action, backed by a plan.

Worry and fear are like sandstorms. They can be painful and can prevent you from thinking of or even from seeing your goals.

But worry and fear, like sandstorms, will soon pass.

KEY 8 – BELIEVE You Are Exceptional

Mistakes and Failures are a Key Part of Success.

It is acceptable to take 2 steps up and 1 step back, as long as you keep going! Thomas Edison said "Many of life's failures are people who did not realize how close they were to success when they gave up."

When you choose to pursue anything that you are passionate about, you are destined to face failures. It is simply a part of the process of life and mandatory for your journey to success. You must learn to embrace failures, not as a flaw in your character, but merely as an obstacle that you can and should overcome. Failures are basically a learning experience of what "did not" work. Not that "IT" doesn't" work. Make sure that you understand the difference.

If you choose to stop at your next obstacle, then your journey has finished. If you completely give up, that is when you have failed. If you choose to keep going you might encounter another failure, but through the sheer act of persistence, you will eventually succeed.

A mistake that is encountered or created with good intentions is actually a positive result. This means that you are doing something, and through doing that something, you have just discovered what won't work. This may sound odd to you, but it is true.

Previously in my career, I had many opportunities to experience this first hand. I remember thinking that I was working, when in fact I was just going through the motions of failing and thinking that nothing was happening. I was wrong.

KEY 8 – BELIEVE You Are Exceptional

Once I learned to step up my tempo and focus on what I was actually doing, I started learning from my mistakes. As a result, I started to perform at my job.

I have made many mistakes in my life. They do not define me. They have created the positive person that I am and they have led me to success.

However, holding on to mistakes of your past is indeed a mistake.

As you encounter failure and mistakes in your life, that little voice of despair will want you to hold onto those failures as a reminder of your past. You must let it go. You cannot change your past, but you can accept your past, forgive yourself and you can write a new future, if you choose to. Think of the mistakes of the past as heavy weights.

Every time you choose to hold on to those mistakes and failures, you are actually choosing to carry that unnecessary weight. Don't let others give you more unnecessary weight in the form of negative words.

A failure isn't someone who fails, a failure is someone who refuses to keep going after they have failed.

KEY 8 – BELIEVE You Are Exceptional

After a period of time, you can see that the burden will be entirely too big for you to carry. In fact, it will start to weigh you down and prevent you from moving forward.

Choose to let go of your past and start writing a new future for yourself. Think of it this way: By writing a new future, taking action on it and actually living it; as time progresses, you are actually creating a new past and better memories for yourself. This will allow you to perform better in your career and in your life.

It is your life.
Choose to live it well and choose to be happy.

Competence Leads to Confidence.

This is all about knowing your product, your company story, your sales presentation and your industry. You need to know, what you need to know. You learn this from watching leaders in your profession, attending trainings and attending meetings with top performers.

When you know your stuff, you don't need to worry about anything. Confidence is a product of knowing your stuff well and being able to execute well.

As I work with salespeople, it's easy to see the lack of confidence in new hires and non-performers versus the solid confidence levels in tenured performers.

KEY 8 – BELIEVE You Are Exceptional

The standard answer that I get when I ask people why they lack confidence is this: "What if my prospect asks me something that I don't know?"
Educate yourself!
Do this because you will run with the full confidence that you are capable. Your confidence level will be high and so will your results.

When you are competent about what you are selling, you increase your confidence!

Manage Your Business Through "Standards" Not "Exceptions."

Not everything in this book will apply to every situation all of the time. I started this book by saying there is not a silver bullet or a magical phrase to help you succeed. However, these Keys should be applied to the majority of the business and prospect situations that you will experience. You always manage your business to the sales standards that you have learned.

Earlier I shared with you how you should always present a proposal live. If your client is out of state and you do not have a travel policy, then obviously you cannot present live. This would be an exception.

KEY 8 – BELIEVE You Are Exceptional

Have you ever worked with a colleague who claims that they "Only work certain type of opportunities?" You know who I'm talking about. You will discover that these certain type of salespeople, usually have very limited success with whatever the "certain type" is that they say they are targeting.

The certain type almost always represents a situation that they had success with a few times, maybe only even once, thus the exception.

They will still spend the majority of their time glorifying over these past successes that are few and far between.

This type of mindset is usually driven by ego and excuses. It is typically fueled by call reluctance and/or an unwillingness to really do what it takes to succeed.

It's easier for some to hide behind successes of the past or ideals of a dream strategy, than it is to really take action to succeed.

What does it take to succeed? The Keys that you have been reading.

There are always exceptions, but
Do not manage your sales process
to the exceptions.
YOU should be the only exception.

KEY 8 – BELIEVE You Are Exceptional

Act, Think and Speak for Where You Expect to Be, Not for Where You Are.

You have probably worked with or know someone in your career who looks and acts the part of an established leader, even though they might currently be an individual contributor or maybe even new to their line of work.
If you can relate to this, then you will understand. How you conduct yourself in all aspects of your current life, will determine your future outcome:

- If you don't believe that you are good enough to get promoted, you won't.
- If you dress like everyone else who is mediocre and happy with where they are, how can you stand out?
- If you talk in a way that leads others and pushes others to do better, you will establish yourself as a leader and you will stand out as a leader.

Eventually you will move into leadership, because you will have established yourself as a leader.

Looking back on my career, I acknowledge this strategy as one of the many contributing factors to my success in business and sales. I dressed for where I viewed myself. I always wore a business suit, a starched shirt, and polished shoes. I was often asked if I was the manager or VP. It was a great feeling.
I enunciated my words when speaking with people and when I conducted business, I was professional. I thought, acted and spoke as if I was the boss, because that is where I expected to be.
In my mind, I always pictured myself as a leader and thought of myself as a leader. Therefore, my thoughts transferred into my actions and words.

KEY 8 – BELIEVE You Are Exceptional

Be a Leader and Set the Example.

Do you want to be accepted or do you want to be successful? How about doing both?

In sales, bonding with your team is very important. Performing in sales is equally important.

Leading is critical.

I'm not saying that you are to replace your boss or act bossy. What I am saying is this:

- Do the right things and set the right example for others to follow.
- Arrive to meetings on time.
- Give positive input.
- Mentor others.
- Provide assistance and support your manager.
- Make your calls and make enough to be successful.
- Don't complain, regardless of the temptation to join in group gossip.
- Run your business in a way that others admire.
- Don't be part of the herd, living your life aimlessly.
- Be a leader, set the path and get the results that others are attracted to follow!

KEY 8 – BELIEVE You Are Exceptional

Change Your Sales Culture.

In a broken sales culture, no one is selling. Why? Because no one is selling.

It is either fashionable to SELL or it is acceptable "NOT" to SELL. Your job is to change your culture for you and everyone else to start selling more. I once conducted an experiment with a sales team. This is how it went:

Scenario number 1-

I asked 7 salespeople in the room to pretend that they were a fictitious sales team of 7 people. Of the 7 people, 6 were to be at 100% or above quota and only 1 of them, Joe, was to be at less than 50% of quota. When I asked the other 6 people in the room, with Joe present, to give their thoughts on Joe's results, this is what they said:

- Joe is dragging down the team.
- Joe needs to step it up.
- What is Joe doing all day?
- They said Joe should probably consider quitting, and
- Some said Joe should be fired.

After I gathered everyone's input on Joe, I asked Joe what he thought of his performance, relative to the team's performance. I also asked how he felt about their input. This is what he said:

- "Man I feel terrible. I'm not carrying my workload and I really feel like I should quit."

KEY 8 – BELIEVE You Are Exceptional

Scenario Number 2 -
I then asked everyone to pretend that they were the same fictitious sales team of 7, but this time those same 6 people were now at **50% or less** of their quota. Joe **was still to be at 50% or less of his quota.**

Under these *new* circumstances, when I now asked the other 6 people in the room, with Joe present, to give their thoughts on Joe's results, this is what they said:

- Maybe Joe needs help with his sales.
- Maybe Joe was working hard but the results weren't there.
- We should cut Joe some slack.
- They now said Joe should not quit.
- They said Joe should not be fired.

After I gathered everyone's input on Joe, I asked Joe what he thought of his performance relative to the team's performance and what he felt about their input. This is what he said:

- "Man I feel good and accepted. I'm right in line with everybody else."

The end result of the experiment was this:
In both of scenarios, Joe's circumstances stayed exactly the same.
It never changed.

In scenario 1: Everyone was "Selling" and Joe felt bad, he wanted to quit and everyone wanted him to quit.

KEY 8 – BELIEVE You Are Exceptional

In scenario 2: Everyone was under producing just like Joe and everyone felt right in line. They even felt bad for Joe. However, now Joe no longer felt he needed to quit, even though HIS circumstances had never changed.

This experiment proves 2 things:

1. That when the majority of your sales staff is not producing, the culture is an acceptable one of non-performance. Everyone feels ok, even though no one is selling. This will lead to less sales without an accountability to sell more.
   RESULT: The sales culture is broken.

2. That when the majority of your sales staff is producing, the culture is one of performance. Everyone feels great about their performance and non-performance is not tolerated and it is not accepted.
   RESULT: The sales culture is performance-based.

   ➢ Are you contributing to a broken sales culture?
   ➢ Are you selling to your potential and to your quota?
   ➢ Are you feeling comfortable because others are not performing to team or company standards?

If so, it's time to break away and start changing the culture.

KEY 8 – BELIEVE You Are Exceptional

"Where you are in your life right now is only temporary. It's up to you to let it become permanent."

(This applies to top producers as well as under performers.)

Manage Your Life to be an Exception, Not a Standard.

Here is the irony. To be an exceptional salesperson, you do not live your life like the many "standard" salespeople:

- Do the things that they won't do.
- Go where they won't go.
- Talk with people they are afraid to talk to.
- Make more sales calls.
- Ask prospects for their business.
- Follow the Keys in this book. Internalize them and practice them daily.
- Find out what the under performers in your company are saying and don't say that!
- Find out what they are doing and DON'T DO IT!
- Find out what they are thinking and DON'T THINK that way!

It is easy to follow the herd, but being a part of the herd means that you are always following someone else. That means you will eventually end up somewhere else. That's pretty scary, especially if you don't know where they are going.

KEY 8 – BELIEVE You Are Exceptional

As a rookie salesman, after I was tired of being a low performer, I started to take notice of the top performers in the office. Their qualities were very apparent and simple enough, but the idea that I needed to take action was overwhelmed by my call reluctance.

The one thing that did stand out to me was the handful of top producers in my sales office of many.

They were the exception.

They were usually in the office before the rest of us "standards." They usually stayed a bit later than the rest of us and they were almost always doing something "sales generating" while they were in the office. Oh and by the way, they were always at or above quota.

They were the exception.

You must manage your business and personal life in the same way: to be the exception.

This book has provided you with the Keys necessary for you to be the exception.

KEY 8 – BELIEVE You Are Exceptional

Seek to Continually Educate Yourself.

With over 20 years of hands on business sales experience, I probably have the equivalent of a master's degree in telecommunications, sales and business, because I have never stopped learning.

I attend trainings and seminars, and I continue to read books like this on sales growth and personal development. I educate myself on how to learn, how to do and how to take action. I research what I don't know from credible resources and I read what I need to learn from books. I ask my mentors for input and knowledge. I rely on the education from those who have it, so I can learn it. I make the investment in myself and I attend trainings and seminars.

You should never stop learning.

You can't.

Once you stop educating yourself, you will stop growing. No growth means no progress. Formal education is only one avenue. It is not the only avenue. With the technology and resources that are available today, it really is your choice if you want to advance and learn.

You have only truly failed when you choose to completely stop pursuing your goals.

KEY 8 – BELIEVE You Are Exceptional

If YOU Don't Change, Your Results Won't Change.

You have learned very profound, strategic and life-changing philosophies in this book, but you must internalize them, so they can become a part of you. Change is uncomfortable. Choose to be uncomfortable for a while, so you can change your results for a lifetime.

KEY 8 SUMMARY

Here is your reality:

You will continue to read this book as you need to or you will not.

You will apply the principles in this book or you will not.

You will internalize the principles in this book or you will not.

You will work on becoming a better sales professional or you will fall back into your old ways.

You can set this book down and baste in the accomplishment of reading a book or

You can turn this into a life changing event starting right now.

Take action and commit to becoming the best person and salesperson that you can be.

Choose to change your life and you will change the lives of others.

You were made to be strong, not weak.

You were made to be confident, not fearful.

You were made to be exceptional, not a standard.

KEY 8 – BELIEVE You Are Exceptional

Your New Beginning starts today……….

Go Forth and Sell Something,
Go Forth and Be Exceptional!

– Mike Rodriguez

EPILOGUE

Selling is indeed a noble profession that you will never graduate from. Do you want to stand in the ranks with great masters of selling one day? Then you must study the great ones and continue to learn and improve your skills and sales process.

To pursue my endless journey of improvement, I have read many books, attended many seminars and listened to a wide selection of training media while in my car, at work and at home. I have watched Zig Ziglar training videos online prior to sales meetings and displayed them at team meetings to motivate and inspire my teams. I have also read chapter after chapter to my sales teams. As such, I have learned to internalize many of the common and standard sales and motivational strategies that have been taught and used by the masters. If anything in this book sounds familiar to you, it could be that you have read or listened to some of the same material that influenced me.

I would like to issue my deepest appreciation and a heartfelt "Thank You" to the following sales masters and true professionals that have impacted my life and helped me to continually develop my sales career.

Thank You to: Zig Ziglar

Tom Hopkins

Brian Tracy

Og Mandino

Jim Rohn

John Maxwell

8 KEYS to EXCEPTIONAL SELLING

NOTES

www.ingramcontent.com/pod-product-compliance
Lightning Source LLC
Chambersburg PA
CBHW071929290426
44110CB00013B/1539